When I Am Weak Then I Am Strong

When I Am Weak Then I Am Strong

A Recovered Addict's View of Christianity &
A Christian's View of Recovery From
Addiction

C J Camp

Writers Club Press
San Jose New York Lincoln Shanghai

When I Am Weak Then I Am Strong
A Recovered Addict's View of Christianity & A Christian's View of Recovery
From Addiction

Writers Club Press
an imprint of iUniverse, Inc.

For information address:
iUniverse, Inc.
5220 S. 16th St., Suite 200
Lincoln, NE 68512
www.iuniverse.com

I here relate my own experience in recovery; what worked for myself and has worked for many others that I have sponsored and/or advised. I am not a professional, but a fellow alcoholic/addict who has "been there" and survived to find my way out, and to happiness.

L. O. C. Registration # TXu001009466
Dated: 06/29/01

ISBN: 0-595-22863-1

Printed in the United States of America

THE TWELVE STEPS OF ALCOHOLICS ANONYMOUS*

1. We admitted we were powerless over alcohol—that our lives had become unmanageable.

2. Came to believe that a power greater than ourselves could restore us to sanity.

3. Made a decision to turn our will and our lives over to the care of God *as we understood Him.*

4. Made a searching and fearless moral inventory of ourselves.

5. Admitted to God, to ourselves, and to another human being the exact nature of our wrongs.

6. Were entirely ready to have God remove all these defects of character.

7. Humbly asked Him to remove our shortcomings.

8. Made a list of all persons we had harmed, and became willing to make amends to them all.

9. Made direct amends to such people wherever possible, except when to do so would injure them or others.

10. Continued to take personal inventory and when we were wrong promptly admitted it.

11. Sought through prayer and meditation to improve our conscious contact with God *as we understood Him,* praying only

for knowledge of His will for us and the power to carry that
out.

12. Having had a spiritual awakening as a result of these steps,
we tried to carry this message to alcoholics, and to practice
these principles in all our affairs.

* The Twelve Steps of Alcoholics Anonymous, as adapted by adding biblical
scriptures, are reprinted with an adaptation of biblical scriptures with permission of Alcoholics Anonymous World Services, Inc. (A.A.W.S.) Permission to
reprint this adaptation of the Twelve Steps does not mean that A.A.W.S. has
reviewed or approved the contents of this publication, or that A.A.W.S. necessarily agrees with the views expressed herein. A.A. is a program of recovery from
alcoholism only—use of the Twelve Steps in connection with programs and
activities which are patterned after A. A., but which address other problems, or
any other non-A.A. context, does not imply otherwise. Additionally, while A.A.
is a spiritual program, A.A. is not a religious program. Thus, A.A. is not affili-
ated or allied with any sect, denomination, or specific religious belief.

"To keep me from becoming conceited because of these surpassingly great revelations, there was given me a thorn in my flesh, a messenger of Satan, to torment me.

Three times I pleaded with the Lord to take it away from me. But he said to me, "My grace is sufficient for you, for My power is made perfect in weakness."

Therefore, I will boast all the more gladly about my weaknesses, so that Christ's power may rest upon me. That is why, for Christ's sake, I delight in weaknesses, in insults, in hardships, in persecutions, in difficulties.

For **when I am weak, then I am strong.**

2 Corinthians 12:7-10

CONTENTS

ACKNOWLEDGEMENTS

First of all, I would like to thank the Lord for the many things He has done, is doing, and will do in my life and in the lives of all those who put their trust and faith in Him.

Second, I wish to thank the fellowship of Alcoholics Anonymous for giving hope and a place to go to millions like myself whose lives would probably end in misery, loneliness, and meaningless death otherwise.

Third, I wish to thank Senior Pastor Dennis Sawyer, the staff, and the membership of **Church by the Side of the Road**. Your love and support makes our ministry, **The Lighthouse Christian 12-Step Group**, possible. Thank you for giving us a wonderful "church home" and "God family".

Last, but certainly not least, I wish to thank my God-sent wife and partner, Konnie, whose love and support are the very best blessing that I have in my life.

FOREWORD

Who has woe? Who has sorrow?
Who has strife? Who has complaints?
Who has needless bruises? Who has bloodshot eyes?
Those who linger over wine,
Who go to sample bowls of mixed wine.
Do not gaze at wine when it is red,
When it sparkles in the cup,
When it goes down smoothly!
In the end it bites like a snake
And poisons like a viper.
Your eyes will see strange sights
And your mind imagine confusing things.
You will be like one sleeping on the high seas,
Lying on top of the rigging.
"They hit me," you will say, "but I'm not hurt!
They beat me but I don't feel it!
When will I wake up so I can find another drink?"

Proverbs 23:29-35

I am told that King Solomon wrote those verses approximately three thousand years ago. They could have been written *ten minutes* ago. They are so very applicable to today and they so accurately describe the circumstances and state of mind of the practicing alcoholic/addict. Apparently, the problem of substance abuse is not a new one, not even for God's people.

This book has two purposes:

1. To bridge a quite unnecessary and unfortunate separation between church-going Christians, who are, themselves, in a state of recovery from sin (Luke 19:10), and those who are in recovery from addictions in twelve-step (and other kinds of) recovery groups, who often feel stigmatized and abandoned by their brothers and sisters in the church.

2. To share with others my own experience, strength, and hope in working the twelve-step program and the joy and love of God that I have discovered as a result.

My point of view comes from one who has been on the "front lines" all of his life; as an innocent child caught in an abusive family environment, as an alcoholic in early, middle, and late stages, and as a drug and sex addict. I know the progression of addiction and the self-destruction, spiritually, morally, emotionally, socially, physically, and financially that inevitably accompanies addiction. I know the denial, the shame, the misery, the terrible loneliness, and the hopelessness that only those lost in addiction *can* know. I know what it feels like to become willing to do things that I never thought I would *ever* do to get that next "high" in order to escape from the reality that I had created for myself. There is nothing else that quite compares.

I also know the hope of recovery from a seemingly hopeless state of mind, body, and spirit. I know the wonder and joy of climbing up and out of darkness and into the light of day after years of terrifying descent. I have successfully recovered from alcoholism/addiction and I have helped many others to do so, not as an occupation, but as part of *my own* recovery.

There is a line from Milton's *Paradise Lost* that I feel defines recovery quite well:

"It is a long road, and hard, that leads out of hell, back up to life."

I've been on that road. I know it well. I feel that I have been called to help those who are still lost, provided that *they are willing,* and to guide them out of the "living hell" that is addiction. I pray that this book will help spread the message of hope to alcoholics/addicts everywhere.

C. J. Camp
6/01

PART ONE: MY STORY

1. Family

I remember when I was in the third grade. I came home one day to find that my older brother, John, had a two-inch gash in his head. It was about one-quarter-inch deep. My mother, who had wielded a croquet mallet, Lizzy Borden fashion, had put it there. She had then poured iodine in the wound. I remember my brother saying that he could feel the iodine burning as it slowly cascaded down between his scalp and his skull. I wasn't surprised, except in the viciousness of this particular incident.

My brother, who is five years older than I am, is actually my brother/cousin. John is the result of my mother's sexual abuse at the hands of her older brother. She apparently hated and blamed her own child for it, yet her guilt would not allow her to give him up for adoption. We never really knew our uncle, he died when I was about three or four years old. I have only a vague memory of visiting him, one time, in the hospital.

The home we grew up in always had an atmosphere of fear and foreboding, which frequently erupted in violence and abuse of all kinds, physical, emotional, verbal, and spiritual. Sometimes, I would be yanked out of bed, from a sound sleep, and beaten for an offense that I may not even have committed. My parents didn't handle anger well. As a small child, I learned to feel the vibrations in the floor when my father walked, so I would know when he was headed for my bedroom door. I still have difficulty getting to sleep or being able to sleep a full night, especially if someone lives with me and is still awake.

Many years later, I learned the real story about my brother's father. At the time, we were told many different stories, but never the truth. The most terrible part of this intimate, family violence was the secrets, lies, and shame that I learned to carry with me. Carrying them became so automatic, that I wasn't even aware of them or of the damage that they were doing to me.

My father was the hardest on me, while my mother was hardest on my older brother. I am told that the vast majority of child abusers are children of abuse. What is clear to me is that my mother took her rage, shame, and guilt out on my brother, while my father reenacted the abuse he had suffered as a child, on me.

I have a younger brother, but he was largely left alone. However, there are two important points to note about him. First, those who are forced to witness violence inevitably become victims of it. In recovery meetings, I have heard others share about regularly witnessing violence in their homes while growing up and the pain, fear, shame, and anger are plain to hear in their voices. I know from my own experience that young boys are especially prone to feel that it is somehow *their fault* that daddy beat up mommy, for example.

The second point is that, while we were small, my younger brother's favorite pastime was tormenting me. That was probably due in part to my staunch independence. I just wanted to be left alone and he wanted attention. This situation was not all that unusual or that bad but for one problem. My little brother was obviously my mother's favorite and she was very *determined* not to see his faults. I believe that my temper was largely created and greatly intensified by her constant and conscious denial of justice, which always left me wide open for more torment from my brother. This went on, systematically, for years and left me with a terrible anger problem of my own. Despite years of working the program, I continue to work on my anger (through steps six and seven) with the help of the Lord, my "recovery family", and the love and support of my wife, Konnie.

My older brother sexually abused me when we were children. He had learned about sex while at a boy's camp that he had been sent to as treatment for the "emotional problem" that supposedly caused his bad behavior. Our mother's abuse and outright hatred toward him, which I believe were the real causes, were never addressed. While at this camp, he was sexually abused by an adult who was a camp counselor. As a society, we were much more naïve back then and such things as child sexual abuse were not discussed at employment interviews or anywhere else. It was thought that such occurrences were extremely rare. I do remember that, when all was revealed, my mother seldom missed an opportunity to shame and blame John for it. I caught some residual shame and blame too, of course. John was nine years old. I was four.

One result of all this was my knowing about sex and having an adult's sex drive many years before I was ready to handle anything that heavy and powerful. I became addicted to masturbation while I was still a small child. I suppose it was a way for me to comfort and soothe myself. As with all addictions, masturbation was both a painkiller and a source of pain (in the form of shame and isolation). My mother, who basically hated both men and sex, was especially cruel in shaming and punishing me for that. Essentially, my brothers and I were made to feel ashamed of being male, and this only fanned the flames of an already-bad situation.

I grew into a teenager who hated and feared women and, though I wasn't consciously aware of that, it had a deeply adverse effect on my social and emotional development. For instance, when I was in my early teens, young girls from the neighborhood would sometimes hang around, close by, and giggle loudly (as young girls do when trying to get a young man to notice them). I would be convinced that they were laughing *at me* and just being mean in order to entertain themselves. It never occurred to me that these girls might think that I was cute or want to meet me. I just didn't think in those terms. I didn't feel at all worthy or eligible to relate to them. I thought of myself as ugly, stupid, and sick, because of the sexual, social, and emotional problems that I had, and because my spirituality was dead. My self-esteem was non-existent. There was indeed "something wrong with that kid" as an observer might have noted.

Matters were made worse by the fact that I could put on a very convincing act that made everything seem fine on the outside. People who have been forced to live in abusive situations learn that as a survival technique. I made sure that no one got close enough to learn the truth. Thus, my need for affection and acceptance was never fulfilled in a healthy way. I believe that is what fueled many of my bad choices and much of my self-destructive behavior.

- *All of this is **not** meant as an excuse.* Nor am I trying to be some kind of morbid braggart. We in recovery must take responsibility for our behaviors, but any picture that leaves this history out would be incomplete and would not allow others to identify with me. It is my fondest hope that this book will show others that, no matter what your background, there is hope for you in Christ and that the twelve-step method of recovery (when diligently worked) *will* bring you closer to Him.

That, then, is the real inside picture of the family that I grew up in. There's more, but that will do. Suffice it to say that my childhood was not what it should have been and all this severely affected my view of the world around me. I became extremely independent and anti-social, trusting in no other person but myself.

By the time I was a teenager, I had built a powerful system of self-protection around myself that, in later years, became a great life-stealing hindrance, but what else could I have done? I probably wouldn't have survived otherwise. As a child of abuse and dysfunction, I didn't know what a "normal" relationship was. I had never experienced one. From my experience, the world was a very cold, mean, and frightening place. As one may imagine, it can be astonishingly difficult to have any true, close relationships with such a view.

As for children, I thank God that I was responsible enough not to have any. Apparently, many people who are parents have spent a lot more time in trying to have children than in learning to raise one properly. There are classes and books out there but, above all, a prospective parent must be mentally and emotionally healthy first. At best, I would have been an undesirable husband and parent while I was "out there" drinking and drugging and all the rest. In any case, I have no reason to believe that I would have been any better a parent than my parents were, though I would like to think that I would have been far less abusive. Still, in that season of my life, I hadn't discovered recovery or the Lord yet.

2. God, Then

Whether we are aware of it or not, each one of us has a "mental picture" of God. Our own conception, which we envision when we pray to God, or think about Him, or whenever anyone else talks to us about Him. Very often, two people who go to the same church and worship side-by-side can, even so, have very different concepts. Some people see God as loving and compassionate and that shows in the way that they relate to their world. Others, apparently, see God as prone to anger and condemnation and that shows too. Today, I prefer the first outlook but, when I was a child, I wasn't given a choice.

My family history had a most profound effect on my own mental picture of who I felt God was and what I thought He expected from me. I tended to think of God a being like my parents. I am told that most people get their conception of God in this way, which is fine if we had good parents as a model. Obviously, some of us did not.

My family attended a very strong, controlling church for much of the time that I was being raised and that also affected my view. Many of the adults in that church believed that the best way to control children is with *fear* and so they helped re-enforce my fear of God. As a result of all this, I pictured God as a terrifying monster; as the ultimate bogeyman who was everywhere, and knew everything, and was all-powerful, and invisible and, in the end, would "get me", no matter what. I could not have thought otherwise. I was told that God loves me, but then, I was told that my parents loved me, too.

I came to think of Christianity as having a God who couldn't wait to punish me, worshipped by people who couldn't wait to judge and condemn me. You might be shocked at how many people have been, and perhaps still are, given this impression as children. As soon as I was able, I rejected God and Christianity and refused to have anything to do with going to church. So, I was cut-off from the very hope, help, and healing that I so needed by my own terrible mental picture.

However, *I never actually gave up on God.* Even while I was drunk or high, I would often talk to Him, if only to tell Him that I was still angry with Him and why. Since becoming a Christian, I have been told that meditating on the character of God is one of the highest forms of prayer. I did that quite a lot in those days. How could I not?

Looking back on all this, I now believe that most people who call themselves atheists are not. I believe that they are just *very angry* at a negative mental picture of God that they have been taught to have. Some say that being angry toward God is a sin. I now realize that if a person is angry toward God that proves two things. First, it proves that they believe in God. How can a person be angry with someone that they don't believe exists? Second, it proves that they have a relationship with God, even though it is a negative one. Revelation 3:15-16 says that Jesus would rather have us hot or cold than lukewarm, and that if we *are* lukewarm (meaning "wishy-washy"), He will spit us out of His mouth! Genesis 32:28 says that the word "Israel" means *he who struggles with God!*

I am thus inspired to think that many people who are angry with God are rather like Saul on the road to Damascus (Acts 9:1-6). He was dead wrong, but he had strong integrity of heart and devotion to his ideals. Could that be why Jesus chose him? In any case, that is more than a lot of people, who are considered to be good Christians, can say for themselves.

Food for thought, indeed.

3. Using

I was still a small child when I got drunk for the first time. My family and I were on vacation, visiting family as we always did. This was one of the few (maybe three or four) times of the year when our parents would relax their guard and all the adults would have cocktails. Each of them would let us kids have a taste or sip of their drinks. This was a practice made acceptable by the philosophy: "All things in moderation". I was struck *profoundly* by the changes I felt when I got that first high! I was free! I had found a magic elixir that made me feel happy and at peace with the world. I felt love and acceptance for myself and for others. Life wasn't so bad with a few good belts in me. I could really get to like this!

Even at that age, I had learned to be a talented opportunist. I found that, if I was careful and timed it right, I could make two or three rounds of the room before I was "cut off". That meant ten or fifteen sips! A small child can get a great high from that much. I knew that alcohol was for me, but it would be a few years before I could buy for myself. How I dreamed of that time!

My usage didn't change until I turned sixteen and got my driver's license. The legal drinking age in that state, at that time, was eighteen. I discovered that, because I looked older than I was, I could buy booze. I wasted no time in becoming a weekend drinker. I would go to the liquor store and get a bottle of cheap wine, usually one of the many "Kool-Aid" wines that were popular in the mid-seventies. I would drink a bottle to myself on a Friday or Saturday night.

I was at a concert when I got high on marijuana for the first time. I had tried pot a few times in the past, but I had never got-

12

ten anything out of it. I bumped into a high school friend who showed me how to use a chamber pipe, which boosts the over-all effect, and it worked. Really well. I didn't begin buying pot at the time, but I would smoke it if anyone else had it and somebody usually did. I really liked the combination of pot and booze, but alcohol was my first choice.

In the early and mid-seventies, there seemed to be a sense of close-knit community among partying people and I really bought into that. All of my friends were drinkers and pot smokers and I began to feel that everyone was doing it. I felt that I had found friendship, or at least acceptance, and a haven from the pain and loneliness that had plagued my life up to that time. I thought I had found the answer, better living through chemistry! I remember the exact moment I said to myself, "To hell with this life I've known!" Just that quick, I decided that I would let go of the last vestiges of caution and pursue what I felt was the only thing that had ever given me happiness. I was seventeen. I had no idea of the limitations and damage that I would be inflicting on my life. I was just a kid in pain, wanting a way out.

Even in the midst of all this companionship, I still didn't date or have any meaningful relationships with girls. Underneath it all, I still feared and resented them. I had very few friends of either sex and I *constantly* had a feeling of being somehow "different" from others. That feeling seems to be universal among addicts of all kinds and, for me, it seemed that there was no escape from it. I could be in the middle of a crowd and still feel alone, hurt, and abandoned unless I could numb myself enough to forget for a while. Those who have been there refer to alcoholism/addiction as "the loneliness disease".

I was still masturbating and fantasizing and I became an exhibitionist. I would expose myself to women my mother's age and then, afterwards, masturbate while thinking about it. Years later, I realized that I was looking for the acceptance that I had never felt from my mother. If such a woman smiled or showed *any* reaction that could be considered favorable, I got a powerful charge from that and so, another addiction was born.

My behavior led to my being arrested for indecent exposure and that led to some horribly humiliating moments, but it still went on for a long while. I felt driven by forces too powerful to resist. I felt as though this were an outlet without which, I would have done something far worse. After I quit that behavior, I saw a television interview with an ex-porno star. She said that many people get into that industry for the very same reasons. They get a big thrill out of being watched because they are looking for acceptance.

My experiences were in the days before VCR's or the Internet, so I didn't see any hardcore pornography until I was eighteen. When I did though, I became instantly addicted to that as well. In the darkness of the movie house, I would sit in the back and masturbate while watching the movies. There was always a contingent of men there who did that and sometimes we would masturbate each other. Most of the men there were old men who wives had died or men who were hopelessly inept, socially. Today, I realize how very tragic that whole situation was.

I finished high school, but in a very sad state and far below my potential in every area, academic, athletic, social, and especially spiritual. I will never know what I might have become and been able to accomplish if I hadn't been so messed up in my head and heart. That is a great sadness. I once read in a psychology book that it is necessary for a person in recovery to go through an actual "mourning process" for all that was lost to addictions and abuse as part of letting it go. I was told the same thing again when I went into treatment for my alcoholism.

I had volunteered for the U. S. Coast Guard during the last part of my senior year, and so I was taken to basic training that fall. In the service, my using really took off. I think most alcoholics/addicts who have been in the service will say that. In the seventies, there was more drugs and booze in the service than on the outside. Every drug peddler in town knew when it was payday on the base and we had our own bar (the enlisted men's club) right there on the base. Concerning drinking, the philosophy of the service at that time was, "Men who *work* hard, deserve to *play* hard." So heavy drinking was actually encouraged. Officially, drugs were not tolerated but they were almost everywhere anyway.

My sex/porno addiction changed from exhibitionism to buying prostitutes and magazines. I would go out every payday and get a prostitute – one that I knew was reasonable in price and not likely to get herself (or me) busted. I contracted venereal disease twice in my first six months in the service. I also overcame my shyness and insecurity (because I was away from home) and I discovered single's bars and learned the art of picking up girls for casual sex. In the "disco" seventies that was not at all difficult if you were willing to dance and "play the game". I especially liked the older women and I was beginning to realize why and admit it to myself. I still protected myself with a cold distance from any real feelings and I left a lot of damage in my wake. I realize now that I was a very angry and hurt young man deep down inside. I was still looking for acceptance but I was never satisfied.

I was in the Coast Guard for three and a half years. I got out early because the ship that I was stationed on collided with an oil tanker (that was three times longer and twenty-eight times heavier) and was sunk. Almost half of us, twenty-three out of a crew of fifty, died. Most of the guys who died were new, just out of boot camp. They got confused when the ship rolled upside-down and all the lights went out. There was no training for that eventuality. They thought that they were swimming up and out of the ship, but were actually swimming deeper into it. That experience greatly intensified my anger at God and the world and that increased my using and antisocial behavior to a new level. I would find out, years later, why God had spared my life.

By the time I got out of the service, I was a daily drinker and pot smoker and I was spiritually dead. I felt no connection what so ever to God or to my fellow human beings. The only person that I cared about was myself and the only thing that I cared about was getting intoxicated. I was indeed a miserable wretch. The worst mistake that I made during this time was deciding to move back in with my parents in order to try going to college. I was also thinking that I could help *them* change for the better! I gave up and moved into my own place later, but not before more damage had been done. The book, *Alcoholics Anonymous*, talks about making decisions based on self-interest that keep putting us in a position to be hurt (Pg. 62) and that's exactly what I did to myself.

The next ten years are a blur of meaningless misery and just "getting by", not really having a life. I dropped out of college, did some time in the army, landed and was fired from jobs, played guitar in nightclubs for a while, and continued to use daily. One very good thing happened to me, I got busted for pot and was put on probation. For six months, I went to Alcoholics Anonymous meetings, reported to a probation officer, went to a psychologist/counselor and stayed clean and sober. I went back to business-as-usual after the probation was over, *but a seed had been planted.*

Ten years, one month, and two weeks after I got out of the Coast Guard, I moved to a large city in the northwest section of the United States. I thought I was going to get a "fresh start". I didn't hear the term "geographic" until much later but that's what I did. Geographic is the term used when an alcoholic/addict thinks he can change his life's direction by changing towns, jobs, friends, spouses; everything *except* the person he sees in the mirror.

I actually lived in the country about thirty miles north of the city and worked, drank, and bounced in and out of recovery, mostly out. Not surprisingly, I still didn't have a life. I went through friends and lovers and continued to drift aimlessly. I went through eight girlfriends in three years because my heart was an emotional blackhole. I made a fool of myself in other ways as well, mostly due to drinking excessively. It is powerful evidence that you have a serious drinking problem when even the other drunks desert you.

The "new life" that I had come here to find was a long-gone dream because I had sabotaged it. Self-sabotage had been a constant theme in my life. In an Alcoholics Anonymous meeting one day, I finally heard the term "geographic" and I knew that was what I had done. After twenty years of emptiness and misery as an adult, I finally realized that my life would not change until I did something different, so I did. I made a plan to save and change my life.

4. The Decision To Live

During the last three years of my drinking, I passed blood every time I defecated. A lot of blood. It had that sickly-sweet smell of death. I knew that alcohol was killing me and I had known for years, at this point, that I was an alcoholic and would die an alcoholic's death. I told myself that I didn't care; that I would just party until I died, like that guy in the movie, "Leaving Las Vegas". God had other ideas.

I remember one bright, sunny afternoon I was driving down the back-roads in the country as I always did after work. I had a bottle of cheap vodka between my legs, as I always did. (It's truly amazing how many hundreds of times I drank and drove, and yet I never got busted or killed anyone. God must have been with me, even then.) I was thinking about my 401k plan at work. I had thirteen thousand dollars in it and I was saving another one hundred and twenty dollars a month, which my employer was matching, for a total of two hundred and forty dollars per month. "Not bad for a drunk," I thought as I drove on, happily destroying myself.

Suddenly, reality hit me. I heard a "still, small voice" in my mind that, today, I know was God (See John 6:44-45). The voice said, **"Why are you so happy about your savings? The way you're going, you won't *live* long enough to retire."**

It was quiet and gentle, yet irresistible and incredibly powerful. My blood froze and I awoke as if from a dream. I had no doubt that God had spoken to me, not so I could *hear* Him, but directly to my deepest mind. I was instantly sober.

I pulled off the road and replayed that moment in my mind a few times, right away, to be sure. I didn't know it at the time, but I was having a "spiritual experience". It was the first of many that I would have on the road to recovery. Through *no effort of my own*, my heart had been opened and softened.

I went directly to the twenty-four foot, self-contained camper trailer (in a guy's backyard) that was my home. I then opened the book, *Alcoholics Anonymous*, and read "Spiritual Experience" on pages 569-570 (in the *third* edition). I had to read it about ten times before I began to actually comprehend it. In the first paragraph, it explains that a spiritual experience is a **personality change**, one that is necessary for recovery to occur (1 Corinthians 2:14).

For me, there were no lightening bolts, no bright lights, no angels singing, no changes in the color of the sky, like you see in some movies. There was just a still, small voice speaking the absolute truth directly into my heart (my deepest mind) and I felt the beginnings of a profound change. I made a decision, right then and there, that *I wanted to live* and that I would do whatever it took to get and stay clean and sober. I had become teachable.

I wish I could say that I walked away from the bottle right then, but that just isn't the way it happened. The hold that liquor had on my life was just too strong and God, as I pictured Him in my mind, seemed too far away and inaccessible. I needed a "higher power" that was closer to me. Something that was more "in my face". I thought about it and came to the conclusion that, since I had only been able to stay clean and sober while in the grip of the courts, I would get myself arrested for drunk driving.

I think there's an important point here for technical, religious-spirited people to note about this:

♦ A "higher power" is not always God. I would learn, four years later, that the apostle Paul says, "**Everyone must submit himself to the governing authorities, for there is no authority except that which God has established,**" in Romans 13:1. My *first* higher power was the State Police!

The officer who pulled me over was a full head shorter in stature than I am. (Not very impressive, maybe, but beggars can't be choosers.) However, he was very courteous and professional and I could tell that he was a nice person, so I didn't feel at all threatened. When he tried to give me my roadside sobriety test, I just laughed. "Look, I'm drunk. *You* know it and *I* know it. Let's just go do the paperwork," I told him. I wish I could have gotten a photograph of the look on his face! I guess he had never before seen anyone who was actually *happy* about getting a D. W. I.

I told him my whole story on the way in; how I had gone to Alcoholic's Anonymous meetings and tried to get clean and sober on my own, but had repeatedly failed. I also told him that I knew that I would get serious help as a result of this. I was never put in handcuffs and I never saw the inside of a jail cell. I blew a two-point-eight on the Breathalyzer. I was almost three times the legal intoxication limit! Then the trooper put me in a room with a table and chairs and I sat down, put my head down, and went to sleep.

About a month later, I went to court and got "deferred prosecution" because I had never been arrested for drunk driving before. I was assigned to a compliance officer and told that I had to find a state-certified treatment program. I found one in town and that October, three months after my arrest, I started treatment.

5. The Tragically Hip Recovery House

I really enjoyed the first phase of treatment, which didn't surprise me. It was like going to one of the Human Development classes that I had attended at college, only much more focused and realistic. There was ten of us in "Intensive Outpatient Phase", which was referred to as "I. O. P." for short. That phase lasted nine weeks and was held three nights a week for three hours per night. It was also required that we go to at least two Alcoholics Anonymous (or other approved self-help) meetings per week. With working a full-time job as well, I didn't have much time to myself and that was a good thing. I'm sure it was designed that way.

My classmates and I got very close to each other very quickly, because we were all in the same boat legally and otherwise. I soon learned not to feel so alone and frightened as I had at first. We became confidants and comforting support for each other because we identified with each other so well and wanted to see each other be successful. There were four ladies and six men in the class. Having women in the class really helped me in further dealing with my fear and resentment toward them.

Recovery has helped me a lot in that way. When a woman would share from her heart and I could hear the pain in her voice and see her tears, I could accept the fact that she was just like me, hurt, frightened, angry, and needing help from her fellows and from God. I finally got the truth through my head, and to my heart, that women are just human beings. They don't have any special powers and they are not evil. More importantly, I realized that most women just want the same things out of life that I do – to be loved, appreciated, and given a useful, reward-ing purpose and place in life.

When the second phase of treatment started, it was a real let-down. I had only one hour-long class per week and this was with people who were not in the first phase with me. I felt like the rug had been pulled out from under me. My fellows in the first phase had become my "recovery family", the only group of people I had ever felt truly bonded with in my adult life. I didn't adjust well to the change at all. I felt abandoned and resentful.

There is no excuse for relapse, but that's what I did. I felt lonely so I started hanging out with some of my old using buddies and I got sucked right back into the life. In recovery they say, "*Change your playmates and change your playpen.*" I had to learn why they say that the hard way. Afterwards, I cut all ties with the old crowd, never to be part of it again. That was hard, but absolutely neces-sary. Thank God I was not back out there using for very long and getting sober again was not very difficult.

I owned up to my relapse and was put on tighter restrictions, some of which I designed for myself. I had heard of something called a "clean and sober house" which is a rooming house, just like any other, except that everyone who lives there is in recovery also. My housemates would know all of my old tricks and they would make it very difficult for me to be dishonest, even with myself. In a well-run and well-supervised clean and sober house, I could get all of the support and help that I needed. Best of all, this support would not come from professional counselors but from my brothers and sisters in recovery, twenty-four hours a day. What a blessing for someone who is trying to stay clean and sober but having a difficult time!

However, I was warned that many clean and sober houses are *not* what they should be and to be very careful in selecting one. A counselor in the addiction recovery unit of a local hospital told me about a house that had been started by two guys who were in recovery themselves. This house did not have a profit motive, which most houses do. I also met with one of the residents who gave me a favorable report as well. It was called the "Tragically Hip Recovery House" and was completely independent. That means that the house was run by the residents who elected a house president (who assigned chores and collected rent) and all major decisions were made at house meetings by group conscience (Proverbs 20:18 and 24:6) in imitation of the traditions of Alcoholics Anonymous. When I heard that, I knew that I had found the right house.

I went to "ninety meetings in ninety days" (as is universally suggested for the newcomer) and built a network of brand-new friends for myself. These new friends were all in recovery and all went to meetings regularly. Even after the initial ninety days, I went to five and six meetings a week or more. Sometimes, I went to more than one meeting in a day. I also chose a "home group" (one that you almost never miss) for myself. These people, together with my housemates, became my new "recovery family".

I decided to put my whole heart into recovery. **I have learned from experience that a person who is new to recovery *must* be *assertive* and *proactive* in working their program.** I didn't wait for recovery to come to me, I went after it. I lived at the Tragically Hip Recovery House for two and a half years, eventually becoming president of the house. I will always love the memories that I have of that place.

The day finally came when I had to move out of the house. I had enjoyed my season there, but it was time to make room for someone else. We made that decision with great sadness in what was to be my last house meeting. It was never intended that anyone should live there permanently. I went back and visited occasionally, but it just wasn't the same anymore. That season of my life was over and I had to look forward, not backward.

The property on which the house was located has since been sold by the owner and there are now apartments where The Tragically Hip Recovery House once stood. Sometimes, progress stinks. In the future, I would love to restart the house in a location where I *own the property*. There's a vision that I would love to make a reality someday, The Tragically Hip Recovery House II.

6. The World "Out There"

I don't care if you've been in recovery for fifty years, if you haven't had to move to a new area in the course of your new life, you've got another thing coming. It was quite traumatic for me. Suddenly, I was all alone in the world (again!) and, for the first time in almost twenty-four years, I had no chemicals to soothe the fear and pain. I was terrified in a way that only another recovering alcoholic/addict could understand. I prayed a lot and went to a lot of meetings.

I moved to an area of the city called the "U-District" because the state university is there. So are many hundreds of rooms for rent. I rented a room in a house that had been advertised as a clean and sober house. The lady who ran the house had me sign some papers to the effect that I would not drink or use drugs while I lived there and, if I broke that contract, I would be evicted immediately. I didn't think that was unusual because I had signed a similar agreement when I had moved into the Tragically Hip House. That's standard procedure for a clean and sober house because it provides strong incentive.

On my first Friday night there, some of my fellow residents had a poker game in the kitchen that turned into a drunken brawl. That was when I found out that the landlady actually had a "hybrid house". I had been required to sign a statement to the effect that I would stay clean and sober, but the other residents had not. I suddenly felt cheated, alone, and very angry. I called the police to quiet the disturbance and to demonstrate that I would not tolerate the shattering of my peace. That was *my* home, too!

Another resident tried to discourage me from calling the police, but I would not yield. I always feel very strongly tempted to condemn an enabler because I have been the victim of that sort of person too often. I was not very popular after that incident but I truly didn't care. (It seems that there is always a price to pay for doing what's right because there is always someone who doesn't like it. Oh well.) I gave the landlady notice that I would be moving and I told her what I thought of her and her hybrid house.

While I was still living in that house, a man fresh out of "detox" came to look at the room. I could see that he was very shaky and sweating and I knew that he was brand-new and hadn't yet had any kind of treatment. He asked me, "Is this a clean and sober house?" In that moment I realized, to my dismay, that the landlady was still advertising that house as a clean and sober house. I told him that it wasn't a clean and sober house and that he should look elsewhere. The landlady actually had the audacity to tell me that she was upset with me because I was hurting her efforts to rent the room. I told her that if she kept advertising that house as a clean and sober house, I would place an add in the newspaper, right next to hers, telling the world what she was and what she was doing. She changed her add. I checked.

During this time, I had been laid off of my job as a construction laborer. It seems that God was reconstructing my life in *every* area, including work. I was out of work for one-hundred and twenty days, so I went to over two-hundred and forty Alcoholics Anonymous meetings in that time. I needed support from people who had been where I was, emotionally and otherwise, and had successfully worked through it. After all, that is the whole purpose of twelve-step meetings. I went to two and sometimes three a day.

In my experiences with so many meetings, I found that there are basically three kinds of twelve-step meetings:

- There are *book study* meetings, where passages from the recovery books are read and discussed as to how they can be applied to our lives.

- There are *general discussion* meetings, at which members pick a topic, such as "anger", "making amends", or "dealing with family", and share their experiences in handling those situations with each other.

- There are *speaker meetings*, at which invited members tell their personal testimonies, in-full, uninterrupted.

My personal preference is for book study meetings because I feel that general discussion meetings are more likely to become pointless complaint or "war story" sessions. I also enjoy hearing a good, inspiring speaker now and then. However, that's *my* preference. A lot depends on the leadership and experience of the chairperson, who is usually a volunteer from among the members, and so the quality can vary quite a lot.

In most twelve-step organizations, there are meetings that are considered "open" meetings because *anyone* can attend, and there are meetings that are considered "closed" meetings because only members can attend. Open meetings are good opportunities for loved ones to see for themselves what goes on. There are also "birthday meetings", where members celebrate their sobriety anniversary days. Often, these are open meetings and may feature a speaker as well.

I have also found that the "personality" of a meeting can vary considerably. For instance, if a meeting is held in a church, which most are, it will often have a different atmosphere than one that is held in a fellowship hall (these are usually called "Alano Clubs"). The atmosphere can also vary according to the size of the meeting and what time of day or night it is held. Another factor to be considered is whether the meeting is held in the city, suburb, or country and, if in the city, what part of town. All of these factors and more combine in different ways to determine *what kind of crowd* is attracted to a particular meeting. I was fortunate enough to have a car and some income, so I was able to go to a great variety of meetings and I looked upon this as an adventure.

In my experience, some of the most rewarding meetings are held in the worst parts of town, late at night, and filled with "low-bottom" cases. It seems almost as if there's this "spiritual see-saw" in the world and the more prosperous people are, the less quality they have in their spirituality and visa-versa (Mathew 19:16-26). However, that rule can be dead wrong and has been proven so on rare occasion.

♦ In the past few years, there has been an increase in the number of Christian recovery meetings and these can vary quite a lot in type, atmosphere, and quality also. Many of them use the same twelve steps that were pioneered by Alcoholics Anonymous but some do not. Christian meetings can be hard to find because, apparently, *they see each other as competitors* and don't network with each other the way that Alcoholics Anonymous and other secular groups do. That's unfortunate. It can also be quite trying to one's patience.

During this time in my life, I didn't go to Christian recovery meetings because I was not a Christian yet and I still had hard feelings toward the Christian religion. That would soon change. I was still growing in my spirituality and still seeking.

I was also donating blood plasma for money, twice a week, because I was going through a hard time financially. It has been noted by "old timers" in the program that often the worst times a person in recovery experiences are *after* they get sober. The history of my life was catching up to me (that's called "the wreckage of the past") and my bad employment record made my job search very difficult. I have come to believe that **God may forgive us for our past, but He doesn't take away the consequences. We still have to deal with them.** While I was living at The Tragically Hip Recovery House, my consequences were patiently waiting for me.

This was a very difficult period, but that only strengthened my resolve. I have never been homeless but I have been very close many times. It was up to me to build a new life from the ashes of the old. I moved from the "hybrid house" and gave up on the construction unions, going to work for a temporary agency that specializes in temp-to-permanent positions. Through them, I landed a good job and worked there for over two years and got some good experience. I also continued going to Alcoholics Anonymous meetings four and five nights a week, building a new circle of recovery friends for support. Though I had been clean and sober for three years, at this point, I still needed the program and the fellowship as much as ever.

7. The Car and the "Accident"

In the course of improving my life, I stepped up in the world of automobile ownership by trading in my "old beater". The car I traded for was a silver 1983 Volvo 240 Turbo. It needed minor work and smoked like a steam engine but it looked great and was a real bargain at $800 plus trade. The smoking went away after a few day's driving but it still burned about a quart of oil a week. I spent another $1500 on it, laboring in love, and I had it looking great, inside and out, and running very well. It was the first truly nice vehicle I had owned in many years, my pride and joy, and I began to devote myself to it. I had also been on a diet and had been working out, having joined a gym. I had lost over forty pounds and looked and felt great. I was in better shape than I had perhaps ever been in. Things were really looking up for me.

I was on my way home from an Alcoholics Anonymous meeting on a Friday night when a car pulled out in front of me. There was no time to react at all. I was knocked unconscious when my head busted through the driver's side window. That was it, lights out.

I woke up in the hospital at two o'clock Saturday morning, not knowing why I was there because I had no memory of the accident. I had really gotten my "bell rung" very soundly. My car had been totaled and I had only liability insurance. My right leg was crushed when the dashboard caved in on it. My kneecap had been split in half and each half had been pulled by the tension on the tendons into another part of my leg. The upper half into my thigh, and the lower half into my calf. The arch of my right foot was crushed, the three largest bones having been broken. The doctor told me later that each of these injuries, by itself, would have been considered catastrophic but I had both of them in one leg! There was some doubt that I would ever walk normally again. I still had surgery to go.

I found out later that the driver who pulled out in front of me was only seventeen years old, yet he had already had his driver's license suspended for causing a series of other accidents. Therefore, he had no insurance. He was also the only sober person in a car full.

The doctors put titanium screws in my foot and kneecap to help the bones heal properly and, all together, this racked up over twenty-thousand dollars in medical bills. Luckily, I had health insurance to cover *most* of the cost, but I was back in debt, without a car, and unable to work because I was in a cast up to my waist and walking on crutches. I also had two more surgeries to look forward to; one each, to remove the metal from my foot, and later, from my knee.

I felt as alone, afraid, and vulnerable as I ever had in my life and that is saying a lot. A lady that I had met at recovery meetings came to see me and brought candy and a card. She said *something* just told her to. Many times, the caring I have needed has come from an unexpected direction. Later, another lady that I had been dating as a friend and one of my A. A. buddies also visited me.

Someone at the hospital found my parent's phone number in my wallet and called them while I was unconscious, so I found out that my father was on the way. That news instantly made me angry, though I didn't consciously know why at that moment. I wasn't at my best. I was very groggy, very tired, and extremely vulnerable. Just trying to stay awake was too much. I figured out a way to go to the bathroom by myself. That was really quite a feat, considering the state I was in.

I realized why I was angry about the news of my father's coming soon after I had gotten some sleep. I owed him money, and I knew that he would hit me up *hard* for it. I had realized that my father had all the unpleasant personality characteristics of an alcoholic/drug addict himself, but he didn't drink excessively or do drugs.

I began to piece together the mystery. I found out from my mother that my father had been paying out two-hundred dollars per month in life insurance since the early sixties. That's the story that *she* was given anyway. That was like eight-hundred dollars per month in today's dollars. By the time my brothers and I had grown, he had paid a large fortune to the insurance company. He had told us, during those years, that he didn't have any money for things that most people consider basics. I also found out that my father had spent over forty-thousand dollars on chances to win sweepstakes contests in the previous few months alone. *Now, that's an addiction!* I know that there is more to my father's financial dealings than I will ever be allowed to know.

My father was *fully aware* of my struggle to rebuild my life. He stood over me in the state I was in, physically and financially, and used guilt and intimidation to get me to repay him while he was "helping me to recover" from my injuries. I didn't find out about the sweepstakes contests until a few weeks later but, when I did, I knew all that I really needed to know. I finally accepted the reality that had been in front of me all of my life. I decided to "divorce" my parents. I have told them that I release them from any obligations of any sort toward me.

My father has an area, deep in his heart that is ice cold and implacable. From my own experience, I know that coldness is the result of shame and fear that are way deep down. Fear is a very damaging part of many people's lives. In a case like this, it becomes a soul-sickness that infects a person's entire life. *I also know that the same enemy lives within me and, without Christ, I have no chance against it.*

My parents refuse to learn or change and they help each other stay the way they are. That is the very definition of the term "enabling". I have forgiven them, but I don't see them anymore. It's just too damaging to my own emotional health and I feel that I would be telling my parents that what was done to me and to my brothers was OK. It is not. I don't blame them for wanting their money, but I finally admitted to myself that my entire association with my parents has been more harm than good, as bad as that may sound.

I had to realize that my family is my *worst enemy* in recovery because they will always try to drag me back into the old ways of thinking and reacting. They don't mean to - it's automatic. Experts refer to alcoholism/addiction as "the family disease" and say that, in their own way, the family is just as ill as the alcoholic/addict. The family's dynamics can undo everything that the person in recovery has accomplished. That's what was happening with my parents every time I had extended contact with them. The recovery rule, *Change your playmates and change your playpen*, must sometimes include a person's family. That is a hard truth, but truth all the same (Matthew 10:34-39).

Some people say that I can't be a true Christian and have such problems with family. That thought has caused me a lot of pain and anguish. I have studied the scriptures concerning this and I have found that Jesus had problems with family and friends also. Consider John 7:1-5 and then Mark 3:20-35. For a long time, Jesus' earthly family didn't believe in Him and they even thought that He was crazy! Notice how Jesus handled it. He stayed with His "church family" and I believe that I should do likewise.

I don't believe that this whole episode was any "accident" actually. I believe that God is sovereign and that nothing happens in God's world by accident. In this time of terrible trail, I had a wonderful and very important thing happen to me. I finally arrived at the place in my spiritual growth where I could ask Jesus into my heart and really mean it and want it. I had never actually done that before. I was back at square one but, this time, I wasn't alone! I had a brand-new life and standard by which to look at the world. I also had a much better view of God.

♦ I feel it should be noted that, as of this writing, I have been a Christian for only three years. God is just getting started with me! I will always have more work to do in my relationship with Him. The next chapter explains better.

8. God, Now

"And we who **with unveiled faces** all reflect
the Lord's Glory, are being transformed into
His likeness with ever increasing glory, which
comes from the Lord, who is the Spirit."

2 Corinthians 3:18

I came to realize that the apostle Paul is referring to the process of getting rid of preconceived and/or mistaken ideas and opening our minds when he uses the words "with unveiled faces". Some Bible scholars translate that phrase as literally meaning "with unveiled *minds*".

I heard a story when I was in treatment about a young man and his mental picture of God. His counselor could see that he was one of those who *claimed* to be atheist, but actually was just very angry at the mental picture of God that he had been taught to have. So his counselor told him to forget all the things that he had been taught about God. Instead, the counselor gave him a sheet of paper and a pencil. He then instructed the young man to make a list of all the things that he sincerely believed, in his heart, that God *should* be. When the young man was finished with his list, he presented it to his counselor who looked at it, gave it back, and said, "Meet God!"

That story has stuck with me ever since I heard it for two reasons. First, before I became a Christian, it freed me to start my spiritual growth with a God that I could feel I was good enough for. Second, I think it teaches a *brilliant* lesson for Christians.

37

Imagine if, when the time was right and he could accept it, the young man's counselor had shown him, in the Bible, that God *does* have all those characteristics! That is exactly what I did for myself.

Allow me to give you one example. I have always thought that God should be just as concerned about *why* we do something as He is about *what* we do. My reasoning has two points:

(1) A person can do a **good** thing for a **bad** reason (such as helping an old lady across the street *only* so that people will see him and think well of him).

(2) A person can do a **bad** thing for a **good** reason (such as hurting an adult in order to prevent that person's abuse of a child).

That was on *my* list; I felt that God should be discerning enough to care about motives. Low and behold! Proverbs 16:2 says, "All a man's ways seem innocent to him, but **motives** are weighed by the Lord." (See also Matthew 6:1-5) By using this process, I was able to prove every characteristic on my list to be truly that of the Lord. However, this process took a lot of determination and time to accomplish.

I had been a member of Alcoholics Anonymous for three years, praying to the God of my understanding (whom I did not give a name), when I began to have a vague sense that I had grown in my spirituality as far as I could. This feeling grew more insistent as time went on and so I began to talk about it in A. A. meetings. I talked about my having been raised as a Catholic but that I just couldn't reconcile myself to the angry, hurtful, frightening image of God that I had been taught to have. Someone told me about a book called *Sermon on the Mount* by Emmett Fox. He explains some things in his book that really began to open my eyes and change my mind about Christ and what the Bible really means.

The part that impressed me the most is where he explains that Jesus was considered a rebel in the eyes of the established church authorities of His day. In the Bible, the established church authorities were called "Pharisees". Unfortunately, Pharisees didn't become extinct two-thousand years ago. In fact, there are more of them now than ever before. Today, that would be the "big time" religious leaders. I feel very strongly that these people would reject Jesus again, if He were here on earth today, and for the very same reasons—He would threaten their positions and status.

The verse, "**Blessed are the poor in spirit, for theirs is the kingdom of heaven**" (Matthew 5:3), is all about that. People who think that they know it all are "rich" in spirit. Another example is, "**Blessed are the meek, for they shall inherit the earth**" (Matthew 5:5). According to many Bible scholars, the word "meek" in that verse means "lowly of mind", in other words, teachable. So that beatitude is better understood to read, "**Happy are the teachable, for they shall learn to make their lives work well.**" A person who thinks that they know it all is not teachable. Like the old man said to the young man, "How are you going to learn anything when you already know it all?"

I now realize that I disagree with many of Emmett Fox's ideas, but he got me started on an entirely new footing with my understanding of God and I am very thankful for that. Mr. Fox's book is very popular with members of secular recovery groups who are searching for more in their spirituality.

My "mental picture" of God has changed quite a lot and *continues* to do so. If that weren't true, I believe it would be impossible for me to progress in my spirituality. I have come to believe that how a person pictures God in his or her mind determines *everything* else (that really matters) in that person's life, because it determines the nature of their relationship with Him.

Our Thorn?

I feel that we alcoholics and addicts who have recovered are fortunate to have been given such a powerful and compelling reason to *keep* working. Some Christians don't understand when I say that I am an alcoholic because they believe that I am condemning myself. I do not believe that's true. I often feel a kinship of sorts with the apostle Paul who had his "thorn in the flesh":

"To keep me from becoming conceited because of these surpassingly great revelations, there was given me a thorn in the flesh, a messenger of Satan, to torment me.

Three times I pleaded with the Lord to take it away from me. But He said to me, "My grace is sufficient for you, for My power is made perfect in weakness."

Therefore, I will boast all the more gladly about my weaknesses, so that Christ's power may rest upon me. That is why, for Christ's sake, I delight

in weaknesses, in insults, in hardships,
in persecutions, in difficulties.

For when I am weak, then I am strong.

2 Corinthians 12:7-10

The Bible never says what Paul's "thorn" actually was. Bible scholars have debated that for centuries. The *point* is that it was given to him to keep him humble and living for God, not for himself. Perhaps it is that way with people in recovery. We must remember that we are recovered, not cured. We must remain humble and not forget that it will never be alright for us to drink or use again.

The "big book", *Alcoholics Anonymous,* explains that all we actually have is a daily reprieve from our alcoholism (or addiction), which depends on the maintenance and growth of our spirituality and that we must each ask daily for the knowledge of God's will for us and the ability to carry that out (Page 85).

Jesus said, "...seek first (God's) kingdom and His righteousness, and all these (other) things will be given to you as well." (Matthew 6:33)

Same idea.

9. The Church

I was searching for more "room to grow" in my spirituality, so I began to explore by going to churches, Catholic, Baptist, Lutheran, etc. I had recently moved to a house located near a large non-denominational church that was a very alive, dynamic church and I started going there. I decided that non-denominational was the way to go since I had no idea of the technical differences between all the different church denominations. I got baptized that August.

I decided that I would apply the basic lessons that I had learned as a member of Alcoholics Anonymous to my Christian training. That means that I became assertive and proactive, taking every class that was offered in adult Christian education: Discipleship 101, 102, and 103 and then Leadership 101 and 102. I even took some classes at the Bible College. I didn't wait for the training to come to me, I actively sought after it.

My Alcoholics Anonymous sponsor (or mentor) got very upset with me because I was now going to church more often than I was going to A. A. meetings. We eventually had a serious falling out and I began to feel like a man without a country. Although I didn't try to convert anyone and merely talked about *my own* beliefs, the people at A. A. meetings tried to discourage me from talking about Christianity. When I talked about recovery from alcoholism at church, I often met with a similar reaction.

I began to realize that there is a lot of suspicion and distrust between Alcoholics Anonymous and members of the church. I believe that this situation is unnecessary because the whole idea for the twelve step process was taken from the biblical teaching of cleaning up one's life (putting off the old self) and learning to seek and do God's will (putting on the new self) found in Ephesians 4:17-24 as well as in *many other places* in the New Testament.

I began my first Christian recovery group at the Non-denominational church that I was attending not long after I became a Christian. I felt so strongly about trying to combine Christianity and recovery. The group didn't do very well, that is, it didn't "take off" and grow like I had hoped it would. Perhaps there are a lot of reasons for that. I had a lot to learn, for one.

A lovely woman that I had met in one of my church classes, joined her group to mine that summer. Her name was Konnie and she had a twelve-step group for people who are codependent. We called the new group "The Radical Christian Recovery Group" and together we had meetings for the rest of a year. We didn't have much success in getting the group to grow past about six members. It seemed to us that most of the key people in that church just weren't willing to accept the twelve-step process of recovery and spiritual growth as being a properly Christian idea. I began to feel that God was calling me elsewhere.

A few of our meetings were attended by a lady who told me about a church where they had previously had a successful twelve-step recovery group, but the facilitator had left. I felt that this could be the answer that I had been praying for. A few days later, Konnie and I made an appointment to talk to the senior pastor. We found him to be very kind and open to the idea. We found out that he had come to this church from the Chicago area where he had gotten experience working with recovery groups such as Alcoholics Anonymous as part of his ministry. He told us that the church leadership had recently been considering starting up the twelve-step program again and they were looking for someone to lead it. What a coincidence! Or was it? That very day the three of us decided that it was a match and Konnie and I began making plans to move our ministry to the new church.

We arranged with the senior pastor to meet with people who had been key members of the previous twelve-step group and the foundation for **The Lighthouse Christian 12-Step Group** was laid in those initial meetings. I had to be firm in my assertion that this would be a twelve-step recovery group and not a church service or Bible study. It seems that there are always those who want to make the meeting a church service or Bible study because that is so deeply ingrained in them. I explained that there is a very serious problem with that.

In most church services, singing during praise music and listening to the sermon are the only activities expected from the congregation. As a result, many Christians become complacent or apathetic to the point that they say, "I just want to be fed the word." Hearing that statement always makes my stomach queasy because alcoholics/addicts cannot afford to take such a position. Doing so all but guarantees failure in the effort to *stay* clean and sober, once that goal has been achieved. Addiction is a powerful, patient, and subtle foe.

In most sermons, we hear a lot about *what* (a true relationship with God) and a lot about *why* (to go to heaven), but not much, if anything, about *how*. What the twelve steps offer is a well-proven method of how. How to let go of one's self-will in order to do God's will, how to rid one's self of addictive behaviors, how to live in the here and now, how to have serenity in times of trial, and how to have a quality relationship with God and others. In other words, how to live as Christ told us we should. From my experience, I have learned that there will always be individual action and an attitude of being teachable, required to accomplish these goals.

PART TWO: THE TWELVE STEPS

10. Step One:

We admitted we were powerless over our addictions—that our lives had become unmanageable.

Principle: Self-honesty

"A man's own folly ruins his life, yet
his heart rages against the Lord."
Proverbs 19:3

It took some time for me to notice that this step actually has two parts. The *first part*, admitting powerlessness, means that I can never safely drink or use *any kind* of mind-altering substance again. When I do, the substance controls me, I don't control it. There are a lot of medical and psychological theories as to why, but the point is that I had to stop using before anything else could help me. For years, I was bouncing in and out of recovery because I just wasn't done yet. There was nothing that could be done for me until I got to the point where the misery out weighed the pleasure; where continuing to drink would have been worse than quitting. That was *my* bottom. I was passing blood, I had no life, I was a miserable wretch, and I was slowly dying.

I was in a race between (1) the moment that I realized that I was powerless over my alcoholism and (2) the moment that I would have died. I thank God that the moment of realization won, though only with His help. Even so, it could have been much worse.

Imagine waking up in jail, not able to remember the night before (that's called a blackout), and learning that you're charged with vehicular homicide because you killed someone with your car. Or maybe you beat your wife and put her in the hospital. Or lost custody of your children due to your abuse and neglect. I have heard such horror stories in recovery meetings and they were *real*. That vehicular homicide could have been me; I drank and drove and had blackouts for many years.

In 1 Corinthians 5:5 the apostle Paul said, "**Hand this man over to Satan, so that the sinful nature may be destroyed and his spirit saved on the day of our Lord.**" I believe that Paul is talking about having consequences or "tough love" here. I am thankful that I had the presence of mind to provide my own tough love. I put hard consequences in my own path and it worked. In my experience, the best way to deal with an alcoholic/addict that just isn't done using yet is to *put hard consequences in their path every chance you get.* For example, if you observe someone leave home driving a car and you know they have been drinking, you could call the police and get them busted for D. U. I. That may sound harsh, but you may be saving many lives, beginning with the drinker's.

Enabling

A lot of alcoholics/addicts have people in their lives that *remove* the hard consequences. They do that by bailing them out of jail, calling in "sick" for them when they have a hangover and can't go to work, making excuses for their embarrassing behavior, and the like. That is called "enabling". According to experts, that is the worst thing that a loved one can do. An enabler usually believes that they are doing it out of love, but a closer look almost always reveals a self-centered motive, even if they are doing it just to "keep the peace". What is *most* disturbing is that the enabler often looks like a self-sacrificing hero to family and friends who don't know any better.

The first time I read the second part of Step One (about my life being an unmanageable mess), I thought that if I learned to work the steps really well I would learn to manage my life again. I eventually came to realize that the second part of Step One refers to the fact that I must *permanently* give up trying to live my life according to my own self-will and learn to live by some other guide.

Studies show that most alcoholics/addicts are above average in intelligence. The same studies show that they are above average in ego, too. I am no exception. I have the same tendency towards grandiose thinking that all alcoholics/addicts have. I think that I deserve more than anyone else and that the rules are for other people. I have heard "old timers" in recovery say, "I've never met anyone who was too ***dumb*** for this program, but I've met a lot of people who were too ***smart***!"

My self-will and best efforts got me to the point where I needed serious help just to make it back from the brink of self-induced slow death, accompanied by acute wretched misery. I had to accept the fact that I will never be able to manage my life without God's love and help. That is what the word "unmanageable" means. My life is still unmanageable today.

That is why the principle of Step One is **self-honesty**. In Matthew 7:21-23, Jesus is saying that I can fool my mother, my father, my sister, my brother, my pastor, my boss, my wife, my bank teller, my teachers, my sponsor, my friends, the police, the courts, I can even fool myself, but *I can't fool Him!* The only hope is honesty and if I can't be honest with myself, I can't be honest with anyone. Everything starts with honesty.

11. Step Two:

Came to believe that a power greater than ourselves could restore us to sanity.

Principle: Hope

"I tell you that in the same way there will be more rejoicing in heaven over one sinner who repents than over ninety-nine righteous persons who do not need to repent."

Luke 15:7

There's a subtle suggestion involved here that I recoiled from and resented when I read Step Two for the first time. How can I be restored to sanity unless I am insane? In recovery, it is an accepted axiom that the definition of the word "insanity" is *doing the same thing over and over again, expecting different results* (See pages 37-38 of *Alcoholics Anonymous*, about the jay-walker). When a person drinks or uses, knowing that there's a good possibility that they are going to get into trouble, make a fool of themselves, maybe injure or even kill themselves (or someone else), and cause serious damage to, or even ruin their own life, that's insanity. There's no other word for it. Like trying to cure a headache by beating yourself with a hammer, it just isn't rational thinking.

As a newcomer to recovery meetings, I was told that in friendships, at work, at church, at school, at the grocery store, at the bank, everywhere I go, and *especially* concerning drinking or using, the same rule applies: **If I do what I've always done, I'll get what I've always gotten.**

Finally realizing the truth of that statement is what caused me to be willing to do whatever it took to get clean and sober. I also knew from previous experience that the authorities would help me, in fact, they would insist upon it. So I knew that there was a "higher power" out there willing to help me (You may want to look again at Chapter 4).

Many people have a very different problem. They claim to have faith in our Lord, yet they don't believe that God will help them because of their sinful past. A careful look at the *Parable of the Lost Sheep* (Luke 15:4-7) and the *Parable of the Workers Paid Equally* (Matthew 20:1-16) might help. The first parable teaches that God is happier about the return of the one sheep that was lost and then was found (like an alcoholic/addict who recovers), than about any ninety-nine sheep that were *never* lost. The second parable teaches that it doesn't matter *when* in my life I came to the Lord. All that matters is that I now devote the remainder of my life to doing His will (and not my own).

The principle of Step Two is **Hope.** I will never again let anyone tell me that I am not worthy of God's love and help! *That is what the enemy wants me to believe* and I know now that it is absolutely not true. Today, there is no doubt in my mind that God (the Father) was helping me find my way, years before I accepted Jesus as my Lord and Savior (See John 6:44-45). This is the primary reason why our "mental picture" of God is so important.

12. Step Three:

Made a decision to turn our will and our lives over to the care of God, *as we understood Him.*

Principle: Faith

"Be still, and know that I am God."
Psalm 46:10

This step is not one that I could work once and then be done with it. A lady I knew and respected very much, who had thirty-three years of successful recovery at the time, told me that even she had to work this step at least once everyday. Step Three actually represents an ongoing struggle between doing my own self-will and doing God's will in my life. Experts say that most alcoholics/addicts are childish, emotionally sensitive, and grandiose people who want to make the whole world do things *their way* (See *Twelve Steps and Twelve Traditions*, Pages 122-123). Everyone is like that to some extent but we in recovery are worse than most, sometimes a lot worse.

There is a story circulated at recovery meetings about a man who was new and having trouble with his program. His sponsor had tried to advise him, but he could see that the new man just wasn't receptive. One day the new man cried out in frustration, "My program's just not working!" His sponsor, who knew that this was coming, looked at him and quietly said, "Why don't you try ours?". The point is that I can't listen well and be teachable while trying to tell everyone, including God, how to do their jobs!

So how am I to know what God wants me to do? I found a good rule for myself: **If it's something that I feel in my heart I** *should* **do, but it's uncomfortable, scary, and not what I normally** *would* **do, then that's what I need to do.** I believe that feeling is the Holy Spirit prompting me (Phil. 2:12-13). That's how He guides and compels me to act. However, I always check with my pastor, my mentor, and/or other people whose opinions I have come to respect before actually carrying out anything. This helps minimize the human tendency to have my own wishful thinking substitute for (or disguise itself as) guidance from the Lord. I must always be careful to double-check my motives and intentions.

The second part of Step Three talks about my understanding of God. I have noticed that some Christians get upset at the phrase: "*...as we understood Him.*" In some Christian recovery groups, they even eliminate that phrase altogether. I think that frequent examination (and re-evaluation) of one's individual concept of God is fundamental to anyone who wants to grow in His likeness.

In any Christian bookstore, there are many good books and study guides designed to help us have a better, more accurate individual concept of God. (I like J. I. Packer's book: *Knowing God.*) I believe that my "mental picture" of God is the most important factor, not just in my recovery, but also in every aspect of my life. I want to be sure that my concept of God is the right one and that it changes and grows as I mature in my spirituality (2 Corinthians 3:18 and Colossians 2:16-19). I know, first hand, the terrible damage that a negative or false concept of God can do to a person's entire life. I also know that a negative and false concept of God can cause a person to damage others.

The principle of Step Three is **Faith**. In the very beginning of my recovery, I wasn't starting from the ground floor in my spiritual growth, but from deep within the basement. If I had not found a whole new way to approach God, I would not have gotten clean and sober and I would never have become a true Christian in my heart. I would probably be dead by now, having died with the wrong concept of God.

13. Step Four:

Made a searching and fearless moral inventory of ourselves.

Principle: Courage

"Blind Pharisee! First clean the inside of the cup
and dish, and then the outside also will be clean."

Matthew 23:26

There's a children's story that I heard once about a magic mirror. I know what you're thinking, but this one's different. This mirror didn't talk or show events far away. In this story, the people who looked into the mirror didn't see their reflection, they saw themselves as they *actually are.* In other words, warriors who thought that they were big heroes saw that they were actually cowards who hid from life. People who thought that they were morally superior to others saw that they were actually immature, self-righteous, and prideful. You get the idea. Step Four is like forcing yourself to sit down in front of that mirror, look into it for long periods of time, and write down what you see. *That* takes courage!

When I talked about having trouble with my Fourth Step, old timers would smile knowingly and say, **"The truth will set you free, but it kicks your butt first!"** I found that there's a lot of truth in that statement. That's the part that they never told me about in church.

The Bible says that John the Baptist proclaimed that each of us should "prepare the way of the Lord", "make straight paths for Him", and "produce fruit in keeping with repentance" (Matthew 3:3 and 3:8). Exactly what does it mean to prepare the way of the Lord?

The book *Twelve Steps and Twelve Traditions* gave me a good, practical explanation on pages 31-32. It talks about my being self-deceived and so incapable of receiving enough of God's grace for me to be restored. It talks about being superficial in my spirituality by (1) giving God *orders* instead of asking for His will in my prayers, (2) not really taking full stock of my life, (3) not making true amends to people that I may have harmed in the past, and (4) not giving freely to others without expecting any reward. In other words, not really cleaning up my life so that God's grace *can* enter my heart. Some may say that this process is not called for in the Bible, but I believe that it is in Matthew 5:23-25, 7:21-27, and James 1:22-25, just to name *three* places.

For me, cleaning up the wreckage of my past life was absolutely necessary. I realized that, painful or not, I had to cleanse my heart (Romans 2:28-29) and do the most thorough job of it that I am capable of. I had to "prepare the way of the Lord" to enter my own heart (Luke 17:20-21). I had to make a searching and fearless moral inventory of my past, not to condemn myself or to feel shame, but to learn what character defects were *behind* my sins. In other words, I wasn't looking only for *what* I did, but also for *why* I did it. That was the primary reason for doing the moral inventory and it was a painful, ego-puncturing process. Here's an example:

I once had a fellow in recovery tell me that anger is actually fear. That statement made me instantly angry because I had always thought of my anger as my strength and my fear as my weakness (I didn't like that guy very much anyway). Later, I realized how profoundly correct that statement truly is. When I get angry, the vast majority of the time it is because I am afraid. *I'm afraid that I'll lose something that I have, or that I won't get something I want.* For instance, when I'm driving in heavy traffic. If someone "cuts me off" it's annoying all right, but if I fear that I'll be late for an appointment, my reaction is much more intense. I can really embarrass myself.

The book, *Alcoholics Anonymous* tells me that resentment is the "number one" offender in causing people to relapse (Page 64). Resentment is just anger that recurs about a specific person, event, or circumstance. Resentment is anger. Anger is fear. That can cause me to relapse, and *that* will eventually kill me! Resentment can be fatal for people like me.

Another manifestation of fear is the need for control. Most alcoholics/addicts are control freaks; we want the world to do things *our way.* This is why self-will is such a liability for people like me. Whenever I tried to control the world I would find out, sooner or later, that I couldn't. It just didn't work. Worse, I would inevitably hurt the feelings of others in the process and they would retaliate. All this made for still more resentments, which are rooted in fear.

Fear! Fear! Fear! It seemed to touch every aspect of my life. I am told that this *self-centered* kind of fear is the opposite of faith and that it is the "primary activator" of my character defects (See *Twelve Steps and Twelve Traditions*, Page 76). It can keep a person from having the level and quality of faith necessary to actually let our Lord Jesus into his/her heart, and that is a very serious matter (John 3:18). I had to be rid of this self-centered fear and anything else that stood between myself and the Lord's grace.

That's the second reason why I had to do an inventory of my character defects, to break their power over me (with Christ's help) by working Steps Five through Nine thoroughly and well. So I needed to make a list of my resentments and have a close look at the *how* and *why* of each one of them. The best way I found to do that is as follows:

1. I made a list of all the people and institutions (schools that I had attended, companies that I had worked for, etc.) that I had a resentment toward. Parents, friends, co-workers, bosses, teachers, fellow students, girlfriends, authorities, etc. My list was pretty long but I tried to be as thorough as possible. For the time being, I forgot *why* I had the resentments. I just listed them (in no particular order). That was "Column One" and took a few days because I started as far back as I could remember and worked right up to the present day.

2. After I had them all listed, I took some time to contemplate each one of them and the circumstances behind it. Then I wrote down the reason why I had each resentment and the emotion or emotions that were *behind* the anger (such as feeling abandoned, betrayed, cheated, violated, or whatever it was). That was "Column Two" and I tried to be as honest as was possible for me at the time. I also tried to remember as much detail as possible, realizing two things: (a) there was no specific time

limit and (b) I would do other Fourth Steps in my recovery life so this one didn't have to be perfect.

3. I listed the area of my life that was affected (such as love, sex, finances, or social standing) for each one of my resentments. That was "Column Three".

I was told to look for *my part* in the problems and pain that were caused in order to clean up my side of the street. I was not look for reasons for blame.

♦ However, I believe that *it was absolutely necessary and vital for me to "feel and deal" with my emotions first.* To get by myself and scream, beat on an inanimate object, etc. Anything else is just *not* reality.

This step brought up a lot of pain from the past for me but I had to do that. Otherwise, it would have been like putting a bandage on a wound without cleaning it first. My wounds from the past weren't healing, they were infecting my emotions and that was killing me. That's what causes some alcoholics/addicts to use until they die. You could say that they have fatal "emotional infections".

It's been mentioned that I have done other fourth steps in my recovery life. Most people in recovery find that their memory improves as time goes by. I was able to remember events, at three or four years clean and sober, that I wasn't able to remember early in my sobriety. These events were too old, too painful, and buried too deep. Nevertheless, these memories were affecting my new life and were the main reasons for the "follow-up" fourth and fifth steps.

The principle of Step Four is **Courage**. I needed a lot of courage but it has been well worth it! I had to "prepare the way" for Jesus to enter my heart. That's what John the Baptist was talking about in the wilderness. He meant that I need to clean up my past life and change my present direction (repent). Working the twelve steps fully and thoroughly is a well-proven method of doing that.

Prepare the way of the Lord!

14. Step Five:

We admitted to God, to ourselves, and to another human being the exact nature of our wrongs.

Principle: Integrity

"Therefore, confess your sins to each other and pray for each other so that you may be healed."

James 5:16

Confession is a very ancient process that has been proven countless times over the ages to help us repair ourselves. Almost all people who are truly spiritual, or want to be, utilize this process. Nothing else seems to have the power confession does for cleaning our "emotional infections" from the past.

I am told that many people have a terrible fear of taking this step. I can understand that feeling. It's so very difficult to trust anyone after what some of us have been through. When I went to my first Alcoholics Anonymous meeting, I felt so vulnerable and frightened that I sat in a corner in the back of the room and didn't say a word to anyone. I felt greasy and dirty and I was sure that everyone could tell that I was the lowest creature in the room just by looking at me. Later, I was told that my fellow alcoholics could tell that I was new and they wanted to reach out to me, but they could see that I was terrified and they didn't want to chase me away. I remember how I felt, that day, when I see a new person today.

It has been my experience that the most frightening steps produce the most satisfying and rewarding results. Step Five was my first proof of that. It's hard to describe the freedom and joy that I felt after I took this step with someone that I could trust; someone that I knew had been through the same struggles. I felt human again, like there was real hope for me, even after all that I had done and been through. I felt that God was with me and would be throughout the rest of the steps. The book, *Alcoholics Anonymous*, lists a whole set of "promises" that will come true upon completion of this step in the middle of Page 75. They do really come true!

Skimping on this step can be perilous, even causing relapse, as something we failed to get out festers and poisons our efforts. We can actually sabotage our recovery, although it may take a while to show. Some people feel that they are the only ones who have ever done some of the things that they have done. In my experience, that is impossible. Others may ask, "Why go to another person? Why can't I just confess my wrongs to God?"

One important reason is that the Bible tells us to. In addition to James 5:16, there is also James 5:20, "**Whoever turns a sinner from the error of his way will save him from death and cover over a multitude of sins.**" This is often the result of confession to a trusted fellow human.

The second reason is purely practical. Another person who has his/her own experience with Step Five can help us stay on track. That means that they can prevent us from skimping on this step or from getting into harmful self-condemnation. I have heard many of my fellows in recovery say, "I am my own worst critic." I believe that is true for many of us. That's why it is best to have an experienced, understanding listener.

The last reason is the best of all. It was so relieving and freeing to tell all that there is to tell to another person and to know that I was loved, cared for, and accepted anyway. I was able to live in peace in my own skin again!

Obviously, the person to whom we are to open our hearts must be chosen with great care. This person isn't necessarily our sponsor, but it should be someone that we can trust absolutely and who understands the purpose and seriousness of what we're about to do. A pastor, a professional counselor, or your best recovery friend are good possibilities. I have been told that it is best not to confess to anyone in your family or to anyone on your Fourth Step list. That may create more trouble and pain for others, which we must avoid. I also believe that it is best not to wait too long between Steps Four and Five. For most of us, that's too much to carry around.

This step can be very difficult and frightening but the rewards are very great. Many people who doubted the existence of God actually changed their minds after this step. It's that powerful! Jesus said, "The kingdom of God is **within you**." (Luke 17:21) He means in our hearts. If you doubt that now, you may not after this step. The truth *will* set us free!

15. Step Six:

Were entirely ready to have God remove all these defects of character.

Principle: Willingness

"A wise man fears the Lord and shuns evil,
but a fool is hotheaded and reckless."
Proverbs 14:16

In prayer, it's easy to say, "Lord, please take away my defects of character." However, God will not take away what I am not willing to let go of. Of course I was willing to let God take away my alcoholism/addiction, that's just self-preservation.

Removing alcohol from my life was like draining a pond on a parcel of land. As the alcohol receded from my life, the other problems that had long been hidden beneath, began to be visible. Would I be as willing to have God remove these other character defects? Just what is meant by the term "character defect" anyway? Let's look at the infamous "seven deadly sins". They are pride, anger, lust, envy, greed, gluttony, and sloth. Perhaps these are more accurately referred to as "motivations" because they are the inspiration *behind* sin. **These are the emotions played upon whenever I am tempted to rebel against God's will** (See 1 Peter 5:8-9).

Pride keeps me from being teachable, from reaching out to others, and from submitting to God or to any other authority. It is this emotion that makes me think that I'm better than some

67

people or not good enough for others and temps me toward even worse attitudes. I still struggle with pride, but not quite so often as I did when I first started working the steps. Sometimes, it takes time and reflection to accept advice that I know in my heart is the truth. It is usually because such advice *is* true that it hurts and makes me angry. Speaking of anger...

Anger is still a big part of my life. I'm very lucky to have a strong wife who is not afraid to give me a good "reality check" when she feels that I need it. I also attend a weekly accountability group composed of fellow Christian men who see to it that I continue to work faithfully on my anger. I do not chair that group. The point is that I must *keep* working.

Lust can be a very subtle enemy. Sometimes, I have to reign myself in from thinking about other women (Mathew 5:27-28). This is where I really have to pay the price for the damage I did to myself in my sex/porno addiction days. I am open and honest with my wife about those days. After all, she has read the manuscript of this book. My wife deserves the best and purest expression of my love for her in our sex life. Anything else degrades our marriage.

Envy is just another word for coveting my neighbor's possessions or attributes (Exodus 20:17). Envy keeps me from being happy with the blessings that God has given me in my own life and that can lead to all sorts of trouble. I try to stay away from most advertising because it is professionally designed to create this emotion.

Greed and *gluttony* are very closely related to each other and to envy. For years, I saw my father devote himself to jobs that kept him completely away from his responsibilities to his family. In essence, our family life was sacrificed to the God of security and status. I have seen what that does to a family. This is one of the saddest symptoms of what modern-day experts call "affluenza". The Bible calls it idolatry.

Procrastination is just a big, college term for *sloth*. I guess it sounds better, that is, more justifiable.

Thank God that I have my Lord and Savior, Jesus! I must be willing to reach out to Him and to submit to Him by doing *my part*. Step Six isn't about being perfect, it's about *willingness*. It's about adjusting my attitudes and being willing to do the work each day, layer by layer, like peeling an onion.

Old timers say, "easy does it, but do it" and "progress, not perfection." That means that most of the time, I will have to be patient and persistent (Romans 8:22-25). That calls for humility and that leads me into Step Seven.

16. Step Seven:

Humbly asked Him to remove our shortcomings.

Principle: Humility

"I tell you the truth, unless you change and become like little children, you will never enter the kingdom of heaven. Therefore, whoever humbles himself like this child is greatest in the kingdom of heaven."

Matthew 18:3-4

People in the world consider the word "humility" distasteful today. Most seem to equate it with being cowardly or afraid to say what they really mean. The word "meek" has an even worse connotation. We must realize that many words in the Bible had a different meaning two thousand years ago than they have today. The *Strong's Exhaustive Concordance of the Bible* defines the word "meek", in most verses in which it is used, as "gentle" or "mild", which translates as "willing to learn". Most people in recovery call it "teachable".

Of all the Bible heroes, Moses is considered to have been the meekest, except for Christ himself, thus the saying "meek as Moses". Moses was certainly teachable and trusting in the Lord, but we know that he did *not* hide from confrontations. As we all read in Exodus, he went to Pharaoh and confronted him many times. That took a lot of courage. Pharaoh was the most powerful man in the world at the time and he had every reason to hate

Moses. However, there are two very important points to note about Moses' bravery. First, Moses only went to Pharaoh when God commanded him to do so and, second, only with God's purposes in his heart. That is meekness in action.

Humility is much the same. The book, *Twelve Steps and Twelve Traditions*, gives us a very good working definition of the word humility on Page 58. It explains that humility is clearly recognizing what and who we really are (as opposed to what we may think), followed by a genuine attempt to become all that we are capable of. The definition most often inferred in the Bible is: *To lower one's self.* This also translates as "open minded" or "teachable". So then, having learned humility as best I could, I humbly asked God to remove my defects of character and I continue to do so.

I think it's important to point out that, while it is true that some people have had *some* of their defects of character instantly removed, I believe that most of us, most of the time, will have to be content with slow, steady improvement. This is where humility must be practiced in the form of patience. Sometimes, when hearing of a miraculous, instant removal of a character defect or other problem, I am reminded of the saying, "All it takes to be an overnight success is years of hard work."

To a casual observer, it may have appeared that my alcoholism was instantly removed one day, but that wasn't the case. In truth, I had been working on having faith and willingness for about twelve years, ever since my first probation. Coincidentally, that is the same amount of time that the woman with the "issue of blood" endured (Luke 8:42-48). If I compare myself today with myself years ago, there *is* a huge difference (Glory to God).

However, that difference has been manifested over years. Working steadily over the years and having trust, faith, and patience shows humility. I believe that is what God is looking for.

When I look at Romans 8:22-25, I think that the apostle Paul is saying that we have already received *some* of the goodness that God has promised us (first fruits), but we must be patient and faithful in awaiting the rest. That is what life here on earth is all about. *It's a test!* This is why we need to develop humility, the principle (or lesson) of Step Seven.

17. Step Eight:

Made a list of all persons we had harmed and became willing to make amends to them all.

Principle: Accountability

"Do not merely listen to the word, and so
deceive yourselves. Do what it says"
James 1:22

I had to give myself some credit that I had gotten this far. It had been a very tough and demanding journey but I was beginning to actually *see* and *feel* great changes for the better in my life. As though climbing a tall mountain, it was helpful and encouraging to look back and see how far I had come. I needed encouragement to keep going and, like it or not, I had to keep going if I wanted to be truly set free. These next two steps were even more frightening than Steps Four and Five had been. Trusting in God and my "recovery family", I began to feel that I could make it all the way.

I came to realize that the key words in Step Eight are "*all* persons" and "to them *all*" because this step is actually about all the personal relationships I've had in my life. I had to repair the damage I had done to others in order to repair the damage that I had done to myself. That was the only way that I could again be the person that God had originally intended for me to be. I was terrified at the thought of having to face all the people that I had hurt in my past. My sponsor gave me a simple but brilliant idea that made it seem much easier. Instead of making one list, I made *three*.

First, I made a list of people to whom making amends would be relatively easy. For instance, my fellows in recovery to whom I owed amends for small things like being late or for cross talking. These people would understand what I was trying to do and I would feel safe there. I also included people from my past life that I knew weren't too terribly upset with me. That was a good way to get started because it helped me have the courage to keep going. Rather like starting off at a dance asking your sister or a girl who is just a friend to dance before moving up to girls that you don't know very well. A simple, but very effective method of encouragement.

List Number Two was composed of people to whom making amends would be more difficult. This I called my "medium" list. This list included people who didn't necessarily know about my offenses. People I had borrowed money from under false pretenses, or perhaps I had laid the blame on *them* for things that *I* had done. Maybe I had taken advantage of them in some even more subtle way. At the time, I thought that I was being clever, but now I had to pay my dues after the fact. My sponsor told me that it was important to give myself some consideration from this point on. I was to remember that I was a child of God and I was not to crawl before anyone or allow anyone to abuse me (*Alcoholics Anonymous*, Page 83). I owed these people sincere and reasonable amends only. That point brought me to list number three.

This list included people to whom making amends would be most difficult. Sometimes, I really had to "swallow my pride" because there were people on this list that I felt had hurt *me* more than I had hurt *them*. In that case, I would have to remember that I was there to clean up *my* past, not theirs. We have to be willing to forgive if we want to be forgiven (Luke 6:37-38). Other people on this list would need some time to forgive me because they would need to see the fruits (or results) of my repentance first. In those cases, I would have to let my life itself be my proof that I had changed. That would take time, perhaps years. I also would have to face the fact that there might be people on my "most difficult" list who simply would not accept any amends, no matter how sincerely or persistently offered.

It was extremely important not to allow myself to lose courage. Now, I needed my sponsor, home group, and "recovery family" more than ever. This would be a true test of my faith in God and my willingness to go all the way (Luke 9:62)

18. Step Nine:

Made direct amends to such people wherever possible, except when to do so would injure them or others.

Principle: Justice

"Settle matters quickly with your adversary who is taking you to court. Do it while you are still with him on the way, or he may hand you over to the judge, and the judge may hand you over to the officer, and you may be thrown into prison."

Matthew 5:25

Having prepared myself the best that I could, I was now facing Step Nine. I had to remember that I was not alone. There could be no doubt that God wanted me to make a sincere effort to mend my past relationships (Matthew 5:23-24). I have found that there are many times in recovery when I have to trust God, just keep going, and realize that I am now doing *His* will and *not mine*. It also helped me to realize that I was doing this more for *myself* than for the people to whom I was making my amends. I needed to open and soften my heart and to remember that the real purpose of Steps Four through Nine is to find peace, at last, in my own skin and to outfit myself to help others do the same. This was the only way that would work, once and for all. I had to face the fact that *there is no easier, softer way. It just doesn't exist.* How badly did I really want this?

Now the good news:

The best and most basic amends that I could make began the day I got (and stayed) clean and sober. Each day that I stay away from my old behavior and my old thinking, I am "producing fruits in keeping with repentance" just as John the Baptist said that I should (Matthew 3:8). However, knowing that the most difficult amends that I had to make would be more direct and personal, I started with my "relatively easy" list. I found it a tremendous help to get an encouraging start before moving on to the more difficult situations.

Direct amends are sometimes very frightening and awkward but many times the reaction that I have gotten was pleasantly surprising. Once they realized what I was trying to do and that I was very sincere about it, most of the people on my list met me more than halfway. That is a real testament to the Holy Spirit! Some of those people really had reason to want a piece of my hide.

There *are* some amends that I will never be able to make. I can't even remember the names of all the women that I picked up in bars, for instance. Other people on my list have gone on about their lives and have moved to other cities and I can't locate them. My sponsor suggested that I not worry about them as long as I can honestly say that I would make amends to them if I could (See *Alcoholics Anonymous*, Page 83). Maybe I will get a chance at some future time, that is up to God. In meetings some people told me that if a person on my amends list had died, I could write them a letter, pray over it, and then burn it. Believe it or not, that really helps.

I was also instructed that I had to forgive *myself* and that to refuse to do so was actually an act of defiance! "Think about it," they said, "If God has forgiven you, who are you to refuse to forgive yourself?" Therefore, it didn't matter if someone did throw me out of their house or refuse to see me at all. I had done my part in accordance with God's will. If I can honestly say that I have done everything *reasonable* to make things right, then their resentment is their problem, not mine. Like the man in *The Parable of the Unforgiving Debtor* (Matthew 18:23-35).

I needed to be honest, sincere, direct, and willing to make right the wrongs and injuries that I had caused. However, I was to keep my dignity and remember that I am a child of God. I owed proper and reasonable amends only. I was not to allow anyone to mistreat me. Allowing that would have damaged them as well as myself.

All along the way, I had to pay careful attention to that last part of Step Nine: ...*except when to do so would injure them or others.* It was very important for me not to cause more harm to others by making my amends in the wrong way or at the wrong time. For instance, it would have been extremely unwise and selfish to make amends to a woman that I had been with, in front of her husband or children. In such a case, it would be best just to let her get on with her life in peace. The bottom line was that I had no right to make my peace at the expense of others. I was to have consideration.

If I decided that it was best not to make amends, I still discussed it with my sponsor, just to make sure that I wasn't lying to myself. Dishonesty with myself now, in making amends, would have robbed me of the very heart-healing that I had worked so hard for. The principle of Step Nine is **Justice**. I had to trust in the

Lord, talk to my sponsor, and go to as many meetings as I felt I needed – plus one.

When it was over, I felt a peace of mind and a feeling of oneness with my fellows and with God that I had never felt before. My whole outlook on life changed for the better. I had hope in my future because, now, I felt that I *had* a future! I had heard that feeling peace, love, and joy, *is* the presence of God. Now, I know that it's true!

Today, looking at others who are engaged in this process and realizing that my experience places me in a unique position to help them, I am filled with a great desire to do so. There is a wonderful emotional reward in helping a willing newcomer and there is nothing more basic to Christianity than to pass on the message that, with God's help and an attitude of being teachable, we can do anything!

19. Step Ten:

Continued to take personal inventory and when we were wrong promptly admitted it.

Principle: Perseverance

"Perseverance must finish its work so that you may
be mature and complete, not lacking anything."

James 1:4

In the Gospel, Jesus sometimes compares a person's spiritual life to the building of a house in parabolic phrases like, "...a wise man who built his house on the rock..." or "...a foolish man who built his house on the sand..." (Matthew 7:24 & 26). If we have done our very best up to this point, it can be said that we have each given our "house" a good and thorough cleaning and we may be feeling quite good about ourselves. We deserve that. By this time, we will have worked very hard and put ourselves through a lot of very difficult soul-searching and "circumcision of the heart" as the apostle Paul would say (Romans 2:29).

However, any housekeeper will tell you that houses don't *stay* clean without a sincere, diligent effort to keep them that way. That is what I had to learn from this step. I had to develop a schedule and a style of regular cleaning and maintenance. This may seem like an easy and natural process, but the idea was new to me and I had no experience.

By the time I got to this step, I was beginning to realize that there is always a little more to do and that this business of recovery is not just a process, but a *lifestyle*. The realization and acceptance of that fact is vital if my recovery is to last for my lifetime. Step Ten is the regular housecleaning step and I found that there are many ways of accomplishing that but they all seem to fall into one of three basic types. I call them "In the Moment", "End of Day", and "The 'Follow-up' Fourth and Fifth Steps".

In the Moment

Many times during a stressful day, I may have to stop and do a quick inventory and correction "in the moment". That is especially true if I'm trying to break an old, undesirable habit (such as being too critical of myself) or when I'm trying to form a good habit (such as giving encouragement to myself). Getting rid of old habits and forming new ones are not easy things to do. Research has shown that it takes an average of three weeks to form a new habit and it can take a lot longer than that to break an old one. I have found that one of the best ways to break an old habit is to form the opposite good habit, as in the example above. This process has three phases.

In *Phase One*, I take notice of every occurrence of a bad habit (I concentrate on *one* bad habit at a time.) When I catch myself doing something undesirable, I stop what I'm doing and do the opposite, with a quick prayer to the Lord and *without* self-condemnation. I also apologize if I have hurt anyone or been dishonest.

If I can keep that up, self-correction becomes automatic. I don't even have to think about it. That's *Phase Two*.

Eventually, the bad habit almost totally disappears. That's *Phase Three* and I *will* get there if I don't give up.

Self-condemnation discourages me and can cause momentary failure to stop me. I need to be reminded of that often, especially at first, because it's so easy to lose heart. That's why I continue to need my sponsor, my home group, and my recovery family. It helps to know that others, even people I admire, have the same struggles that I do.

End of Day

I do this inventory just before I go to sleep and I make it a part of my nightly prayers. God is a great listener! There's a wonderful paragraph on Page 86 of the book, *Alcoholics Anonymous* that contains a list of questions for this purpose. It was helpful to me to reword and rewrite the questions as a numbered list, which I could review as part of my evening meditation and prayer. This was the result:

1) Was I resentful, selfish, dishonest, or afraid?
2) Do I owe an apology?
3) Have I kept something to myself that should be discussed with another person at once?
4) Was I kind and loving toward all?
5) What could I have done better?
6) Was I thinking of myself most of the time or was I thinking of what I could do for others?
7) What were the *good* things that I did, said, and thought today that I can be proud and happy about? (Doing this inventory is one thing that I deserve credit for.)

This list can be added to or modified but it makes a great start. I think it's necessary to frequently remind myself to give myself credit for the good things that I do everyday. We all need affirmation and validation.

The "Follow-up" Fourth and Fifth Steps

This is what it sounds like. It can be done on an annual or semi-annual basis or whenever I am going through a trying time. I find that reviewing the chapters on the Fourth and Fifth Steps is a good idea here. It helps to refresh my memory on the basics. These subsequent inventories and admissions are much easier than the originals were because I have experience with the process now and it doesn't seem so strange and scary as it once did.

I will never be perfect in this life. Therefore, I need to have a regular look at myself in order to *keep* my life in alignment with God's will for me. This may sometimes be painful and inconvenient, but I think that this *is* the easier, softer way. Look at the alternative.

20. Step Eleven:

Sought through prayer and meditation to improve our conscious contact with God, *as we understood Him*, praying only for knowledge of His will for us and the power to carry that out.

Principle: Spirituality

"The lamp of the Lord searches the spirit of
a man; it searches out his inmost being."

Proverbs 20:27

One of the kindest, most loving, and deeply spiritual people that I have ever known was a Catholic priest named Father O'Reilly. I was a very angry fourteen-year-old youth and sometimes he would get frustrated with me and my self-centered, vacuum cleaner mentality. Anyone would have. When he'd reached his limit he would say to me, "God always answers your prayers, it's just that sometimes the answer is **NO!**" He had a way of explaining things that was very simple and clear. Everyone loved him and I wish that I could have learned more from him, but my mind was closed. Even so, my memory of him is an example for me today.

I was thirty-seven years old when I got clean and sober and I didn't know how to pray. All that I really knew how to do was repeat prayers that I had been taught to memorize. One such prayer was the blessing that I sometimes heard before meals on special occasions or when we had guests. It went like this:

"Bless us, Oh Lord, in these, thy gifts, which we are about to receive from thy bounty, through Christ, our Lord, Amen."

I'm sure that prayer is familiar to many people, especially to those who were raised Catholic as I was. It's a standard. It is only one of many prayers such as the "Hail Mary" or the "Act of Contrition" that were redundantly and mercilessly repeated. Except for the rare appearance of a person like Father O'Reilly, there never seemed to be any sincere feelings in those prayers. We recited them like robots.

Speaking words that have no sincerity behind them is what Jesus means by the term "vain repetitions" (Matthew 6:7). I had worked hard in Steps One, Two, and Three to establish a genuine relationship with God and *that* eventually lead me to becoming a Christian (John 6:44-45). Now, I have to work daily to improve that relationship because that is what the concept of "conscious contact" is all about. **One of the few things that God will not forgive us for is refusing to have a relationship with Him.** Therefore, in seeking to establish one that is true, I realized that I had to step out on my own and not hide behind a pastor, sponsor, or any other mentor.

The second half of Step Eleven says that we should pray *only* for the knowledge of God's will for us and the power to carry that out. I feel that is what Jesus meant when He said, "...**seek first the kingdom of God and His righteousness...**" (Mathew 6:33). That was Jesus' way of saying "first things first".

Besides reciting memorized prayers like a robot, the only *other* thing that I knew how to do in prayer was list the things that I wanted for myself. That list now seems endless and hopelessly self-centered. I would pray, "Give me a car", or "Give me a better job", or "Give me a pretty girlfriend." Give me! Give me! Give me! No wonder God tuned me out!

In addition to my self-centered attitude, God may have denied me because He could see that I would destroy myself if He gave me what I demanded. For example, suppose I had prayed for a million dollars. Imagine an alcoholic/addict run wild with a million dollars! I doubt that I would have survived.

By contrast, all of the great Bible heroes made it their purpose to put service to God first, then their fellows, and themselves last. Abraham even stood before God and *questioned* Him! (Genesis 18:22-23). I believe that God allowed that because Abraham's concern was for others; there was no self-centered motive. In Proverbs 16:2, it is made clear that God looks at our intentions very closely, so I mustn't try to fool myself about my true motives.

I find it helpful to ask the Lord for His guidance and help in knowing how to have the right attitude. I frequently ask, "Lord, teach me what you want me to know; show me how to be the best disciple I can be." There are those who warn me against asking that by saying, "Be careful what you pray for, you might get it." I feel that type of thinking shows fear instead of faith and it is riddled with self-centeredness. God has a wonderful plan for each one of us. It's all a question of being willing and teachable.

Meditation

I have found that one of the best meditation methods is to carefully consider those sections of Steps Three and Eleven that say, "…God, *as we understood Him*…" A review of that section of Step Three might be helpful. As I have stated earlier in this book, I have been told that meditating on the character and personality of God is one of the highest forms of prayer. I was very happy to learn that because I had always done so, if only because I was trying to figure out why God didn't give me the things I demanded. (My relationship with God has not always been marked by a proper attitude on my part, but I have always tried to be honest with Him.) Once again, I highly recommend J. I. Packer's book, *Knowing God.*

For pure relaxation, another method that I use is to take a "mental vacation". I picture myself far away from my troubles in a cabin (like one of those in Thomas Kinkade's paintings) in the forest during a gentle rainfall. I imagine that I can hear the raindrops hitting the shingle roof as I sit by the warm fireside. Perhaps you would prefer the beach, or the mountains, or a sailboat. The possibilities are as endless as one's imagination. The point is that during a time of great stress, meditation can be a real lifesaver. There are many good books available on the subject. We just need to be patient and persistent. Our abilities will grow and so will the rewards.

21. Step Twelve:

Having had a spiritual awakening as the result of these steps, we tried to carry this message to others, and to practice these principles in all areas of life.

Principle: Service to Others

"If I have the gift of prophesy and can fathom all mysteries and all knowledge, and if I have faith that can move mountains, but have not love, I am nothing."

1 Corinthians 13:2

It took some time for me to notice that this step actually has *three* parts:

Part One is a chance to really look closely at my spiritual awakening (or personality change) to be sure that I am doing the best that I can in utilizing it to change my daily life for the better. The book, *Alcoholics Anonymous*, explains that I cannot pass on something that I, myself, don't have (Page 164). So I must be reasonably sure that I am going to be passing on quality to those that I would help. In the Gospel, Jesus *commanded* His disciples not to depart from Jerusalem until they had received power from the Holy Spirit (on the Day of Pentecost) in Acts 1:8. Jesus didn't want them to leave and become His witnesses to others until they could be sure that they had quality and completeness. Following the same principle, I had to ask myself some hard questions before I began to work with others:

- ◆ Have I been as honest as I am able to be?
- ◆ Have I been as thorough as possible?
- ◆ Have I put forth the very best effort of which I am capable?
- ◆ Am I truly a good example to my fellows?

If I can earnestly say "yes" with a clear conscience, then I am ready to pass on the message in more ways than just sharing at recovery meetings. The other reason for this double-checking is that I **will pass on what I *do* have!** I want to be sure that I am passing on honesty, thoroughness, and quality in my own program.

Part Two of this step is actually carrying the message. There are many ways of carrying the message, but the best way is to make my own life an example in such a way that others will want what they see in me. A well-loved pastor used to tell his students, "Teach the Gospel wherever you go and, if necessary, use words." Whether I am carrying the message of the Gospel to so-called "normal" people or the message of sobriety to alcoholics/addicts, I need to be an example of it.

Being a sponsor is another excellent way of carrying the message. Anyone who has successfully worked through the steps has a lot of valuable experience to share and we owe it to our fellows to do that. That is the best way we can repay those who helped us when we were new. After all, a sponsor is just a friend who has been there.

At meetings, I feel that I need to make an effort to introduce myself to newcomers and try to make them feel welcome, comfortable, and accepted. I feel that I should introduce them to others, give those *of the same sex* my phone number, and make myself available to help them with any questions or problems that I myself have had. I remember what it was like being new. Those feelings of fear, shame, vulnerability, lack of hope, and worthlessness that kept me isolated from the very people who could help me.

From my experience, few things offer the satisfaction of knowing that I have truly helped someone get through another of those terribly trying first days. Then to see those new people grow and change their lives for the better; to see families restored to trust, security, and happiness are very gratifying experiences indeed. However, I must keep in mind that the glory belongs to God, *I didn't do it.*

Nor should I feel shame or blame if my efforts fail with a new person. Sometimes the new person isn't willing to do the work because they haven't hit their "bottom" and they just aren't done using yet. Experience may teach me to discern those situations to a point, but I must never use that as an excuse not to try. If someone that I am trying to help seems determined not to try, I don't waste any more time on him. That is terribly unfair to the person who *wants* to do the work. A good prospect calls his sponsor, goes to the suggested "ninety meetings in ninety days", and does the homework and footwork.

I have often found it helpful to bear in mind that the primary reason for helping others is that doing so helps *me* to grow and stay clean and sober. The best way to get a lesson firmly in my own head is to teach it to someone else (Philemon 6). That reason may seem a little shallow to some, but it is very powerful and it helps me to keep proper perspective when my best efforts with a newcomer fail.

If I am called to go to someone's home, to jail, to the hospital, or to do an intervention, that is an example of twelve-stepping in the most formal sense. I feel that reading and studying the chapter "Working with Others" on Page 89 of *Alcoholics Anonymous* before doing this work, on each occasion, is a great idea. In some rare cases, this work can be very ugly and even dangerous. Old-timers advise that one should always do this kind of work with a partner or, better still, in a group led by someone with experience.

Part Three of this step is to "practice these principles in all areas of life". In Step One, I admitted that I was powerless over my alcoholism/addiction and that my life is unmanageable. I am powerless over the company I work for, the family I grew up in, the church I go to, my spouse, my boss, children, co-workers, mentors, and so on. In short, I am actually powerless over *life*.

Therefore, I must practice the principles of self-honesty, hope, faith, courage, integrity, willingness, humility, accountability, justice, perseverance, spirituality, and service to others in all areas of my life. At home, at work, at the bank, at the grocery store, at church, at the gym, wherever I go. That's no small order! The good news is that I have the rest of my life to practice and that the Holy Spirit will be there as my counselor, teacher, and reminder (John 14:26).

The Serenity Prayer has a lot of application here, for instance:

♦   **"God grant me the serenity to accept the things I cannot change…"** can refer to the fact that I can't change the *company* that I work for.

♦   However, if I have courage and faith as in **"the courage to change the things I can…"**, I can change the fact that I work for *that* company.

♦   Nevertheless, I must also realize that I will always be powerless over other people, places, and things and in order to have **"…the wisdom to know the difference"**, I must acknowledge that God is in charge and I'm not (Proverbs 3:5-6).

I need to always do God's will (not mine) in my life, one day at a time. I also need to check with my pastor, sponsor, or someone else that I can respect before making major decisions, because **God works through other people**. That is the only way my life can ever be manageable.

PART THREE

22. The Christian and the Addict

When asked why I was clean and sober for almost four years before I became a Christian, I like to tell a story that I call "The Parable of the Bus Stop". It goes like this:

When seeing two people emerge from a bus at a bus stop, one might assume that they have both traveled the same distance because they have both arrived at the same place and have done so at the same time. On the surface, that seems like a perfectly reasonable conclusion. However, what we may fail to realize is that the first person was on the bus for only the past two or three miles, while the second person was on two previous buses in the past hour and has traveled across the city. In other words, *they didn't start from the same place.*

It is much the same way with spiritual growth. We can't judge fairly where a person is now, at this time in his/her spiritual walk, until we know how far that person has come. That's why only God can judge us and He does so by our hearts, by what is deep within us (Proverbs 20:27), not by appearances or circumstances. In my own case, I had to work very hard just to get to the point where most of my fellow Christians started.

Sometimes, I have to struggle with painful, judgmental statements, that I hear from people who have been Christians since they were small children, concerning recovery from alcoholism/drug addiction. One example that comes to mind happened to me while I was in a class in Bible College. The pastor/teacher was leading a group discussion and asked each of us to give an example of Christ's healing from our own experience. I offered the fact of my having been relieved of my obsession for alcohol.

The pastor/teacher's reply was, "I don't consider that to have been a healing. I believe that was actually a simple change in lifestyle. However, I do commend you for it."

The unspoken assumption being that I was simply deficient in my moral character and not ill or damaged in any way and, therefore, not actually in need of healing. That mentality is only too common. It is important to realize that many people have been victims of something that has been called "spiritual abuse" or "toxic religion". That means that they have been badly misunderstood, stigmatized, and abandoned *even by their leaders* in the church. The reasoning and belief behind this mistreatment seems to be, **"If you had stronger, better faith in God, then you would never have had any of these problems."**

The predictable result is that many people in recovery have a terrible attitude and much fear about going to church and many people in church, who have recovery issues in their lives, suffer in isolation and silence because they are terrified of the possible consequences of seeking help. I have heard it said, as a joke, *"Christians kill their wounded."* The fact is that sometimes they do and it is not funny. That fact has done much damage to the church.

Another problem seems to be a tendency among church members to "spiritualize" their own troubles and avoid personal responsibility for the truth by using Christian code words and catch phrases. This thinking seems to boil down to a kind of "one-two punch" method of avoiding responsibility:

- "I don't have to work on my willingness or self-honesty to be rid of my problems, because Jesus did all the work for me," would be the first punch. And then:

- "I'm not responsible for my misbehavior because 'the enemy' made me do it," would be the second punch.

The Bible plainly says that I *must* receive Jesus Christ as my *Lord* as well as my Savior, but I have not found it to say *anywhere* that this is *all* that I have to do. On the contrary, there are many verses that warn otherwise. For instance, there is Matthew 7:21-27, which I like to refer to as "the 'Lord, Lord' speech". I believe that passage is very clear and the letters are in red. I especially like Eugene H. Peterson's *The Message* version of verses 21-23.

On the other hand, there is no excuse for people in recovery to refuse to grow in their spirituality. I saw a movie a few months ago in which there was a conversation that took place between two inmates in prison. One inmate asked the other what the word "institutionalized" means. His friend explained that "institution-alized" is the word that experts use when a person not only gets *used* to the walls of confinement in a prison, but actually becomes terrified of life *without* them. I believe that many people in secular recovery organizations have institutionalized themselves in regard to their spiritual growth. It seems that they feel "safe" with their current level of spiritual awareness and will fight *any effort* to expand their horizons. Most people feel that way to some extent, but it's been said that alcoholics/addicts, as a group, are worse than most. From what I have seen in myself and heard from many others, I believe that's true.

I have seen many encouraging signs that churches are changing, but my estimate is that they have about fifty years of catching up to do. That is quite a lot. However, there is a lot of reason to have hope in the future and there is a lot of work to do. In my experience, fledgling Christian recovery groups have very little real chance to survive the necessary "long haul" without strong support from the pulpit. In the past, that has been difficult to obtain, which is unnecessary and sad.

The fact is that the principles *behind* the twelve-step method of recovery came from the Bible where cleaning up one's past life is very strongly taught (See Romans 2:17-29, Ephesians 4:22-32, and Philippians 2:12-13). The twelve-step process originally came from Alcoholics Anonymous, which was co-founded by *two Christians* named Bill Wilson and Dr. Bob Smith. The birth of that fellowship is said to date from Dr. Bob's first day of permanent sobriety, June 10th, 1935. However, the first edition of Alcoholics Anonymous' main guidebook, *Alcoholics Anonymous*, wasn't published until 1939. For the first four years, the text that was used for their meetings was the *King James Bible*. Many A. A. members are surprised when they hear that. The very same Bible that Bill and Dr. Bob used is still on display in a glass case in Dr. Bob's house, which has been restored and preserved in the city of Akron, Ohio, birthplace of Alcoholics Anonymous.

It is my belief that, like it or not, churches and recovery groups are siblings in lineage and in purpose. I feel that they should work together because drugs and alcohol don't care which church you go to or if you go at all. Come to think of it, neither did Jesus.